The Individual & Society

Universal Utopia

By

Tom Noel-Morgan

2012 A.D.

REVISED 1ST EDITION

Copyright © 2012-2020 by T. Noel-Morgan

All rights reserved.

ISBN-13: 978-1492890256

ISBN-10: 1492890251

FABULATORIUM

PREFACE

Universal Utopia is a work of reflection on the course that contemporary consumer society is taking with regards to moral flexibility, ethics, relativism and the surrender of personal conscience. The work approaches the fabric of modern-day global society with a critical eye on how we have geared ourselves for consumerism at the expense of our traditional values, our humanity, our individuality and our planet.

I don't own the truth, but I occasionally borrow it. I will dare submit to you that this work is worth your time to read it. If nothing else, you can criticise it to your heart's content and reinforce your own convictions. After all, this is not a scientific publication, nor is it a political statement. This is a vision. It is an idea as permeable to your scrutiny as you may want it to be. If you like, you may consider it fiction; an opinion from a mere delusional idealist.

I'm not a scientist, nor am I a sociologist or anthropologist. I'm just a man trying to make sense of the world that we face today. I've been formally trained in Social Communications, Marketing and Advertising. I've been informally trained in numerous other disciplines. I do have extensive industrial market experience, a fair dose of consumer market experience, and I can boast some skill in dealing with the public sector and with Corporate Social Responsibility.

More importantly, I have eyes and ears and I witness the world around me attentively. It is upon my observations of the tendencies that I see growing around all of us that I base the content of this work.

Besides, we all know society is not perfect, but is it at least what it promised it would be? Has trading off our cultural identity for relativism and the ethos of profit really bought us greater harmony? Will consumerism ever bring about personal happiness? Hard questions are the questions really worth answering.

* * * * * * *

Timothy 6:9-10 - But those who desire to be rich fall into temptation and a snare, and into many foolish and harmful lusts which drown men in destruction and perdition. For the love of money is a root of all kinds of evil, for which some have strayed from the faith in their greediness, and pierced themselves through with many sorrows.

Matthew 6:24 & 33 - No one can serve two masters; for either he will hate the one and love the other, or else he will be loyal to the one and despise the other. You cannot serve God and greed. Therefore I say to you, do not worry about your life, what you will eat or what you will drink; nor about your body, what you will put on. Is not life more than food and the body more than clothing? But seek first the kingdom of God and His righteousness, and all these things shall be added to you.

INDEX

PREFACE	- 2 -
INTRODUCTION	- 6 -
THE COLOUR OF DEMOCRATIC RELATIVISM	- 14 -
INSATIABILITY & GREED	- 34 -
THE ETHICS OF PROFIT	- 55 -
CURBING THE GOLDEN RULE	- 70 -
RETURN TO VIRTUE ETHICS	- 88 -
THE QUESTION OF CONSCIENCE	- 100 -
THE UNIVERSAL UTOPIA	- 112 -
CHANGING THE WORLD	- 142 -
FINAL CONSIDERATIONS	- 149 -
READ ALSO	- 154 -
ABOUT THE AUTHOR	- 153 -
END NOTES	- 155 -

* * * * * * *

Chapter I

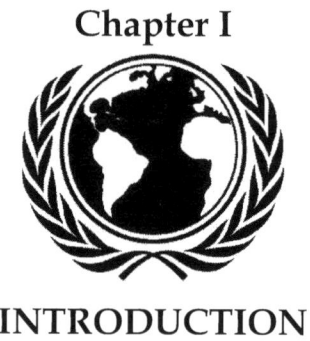

INTRODUCTION

Oh, what a marvel it would be to find the whole world renewed, redeemed and crisp with hope and a true "brotherhood of man" to populate it. Is it such a distant dream to aspire to global harmony? Not at all, for all the impediment that we today struggle withal is of our own making.

Our cradle, the Earth, is not only the birthplace of mankind; it is also our home and our garden. For all practical intents and purposes, as long as we treat it as such, it will remain so. Likewise, society is a product of our imaginations and our efforts. As such, we can devise it to be as we wish it.

As you can see, hope is the birth of enterprise and industry. It is the power that motivates and nurtures the will to build, to make and to change. As long as there is hope there is will, and where there's a will there's a way.

Imagine, if you will, a world where a man is not the sum of his belongings, but of his accomplishments. Imagine a society where higher station is awarded to those people, who serve communities out of altruism, not for personal gain. Imagine an economy that sees profit as a consequence of benefits provided by the seller to the buyer, rather than the opposite. Imagine a world that does not lie to itself, saying that we have pursued the only possible course of action, and that this sole alternative will necessarily culminate in self-annihilation.

These are not new dreams, but ancient ones. We chose to ignore them because we allowed ourselves to be convinced that the dream was impossible. By this assumption, we have allowed ourselves to accept the unacceptable. We have allowed ourselves to look onto our hungering brother and let him starve. We have chosen to let ourselves be corrupted and seduced by greed, convenience and comfort, at the steep price of human suffering.

Compliance, indolence and defeatism have no place where hope will build a future. They are there merely to support the past and make the present endure. These are the tools of the comfortable, the forceful and of the oppressing. It is the means to promulgate the status quo; the way to extend the current state of affairs. Had we reached perfection as a society, then maybe they'd be to the benefit of all.

We have told ourselves that the Earth is incapable of giving humankind what it needs, but have we been honest about it? Have we? Is it Nature that can't support Man or is it Man's own ambition that inhibits our economies from sustaining every citizen with dignity?

No, I'm no socialist. I just believe that we have yet to find a fair balance to our newly found global economy. Ask yourself: When people starve in our time, is it really because the forces of Nature have dealt a lethal blow, or is it because grain and other foodstuffs are valuable commodities negotiated under the ethics of profitability? When governments subsidise crops, do they do it so as to make them more plentiful and accessible to the people, or do they do it to lower the price of imports and exports? These are questions of conscience as much as they are practical problems.

There are many more such questions and very few people asking them. They are as uncomfortable as they are necessary. For example: Do we all need luxury? Do we all need opulence and excess? Is the high-living of the rich and famous the necessary objective of every individual? The premise of consumerism says it is so, but is that the truth? What are the consequences of generalised intemperance? There certainly are consequences.

Make no mistake: The Earth is perfectly capable of sustaining mankind, as long as each of us renounces their self-servitude and the path of hedonist bliss. It is not our ecology and our natural resources that are at fault. It is not the size of our populations. It is indeed the fact that we individually want more than we need. It is the fact that there are those among us, who want more than they deserve.

I'm not talking about a path of poverty and want, for that path is well known in our history and even today. I am talking about the valorisation of austerity, frugality and modesty. I am referencing the seeking of happiness through our choices and achievements, rather than seeking consolation through use of material goods. I am talking about our God-given right to bliss without the need for continuous self-gratification, but with gratification coming from greater things. I am talking about a life of freedom beyond the bonds of consumer society.

I'm certain this is a highly unpopular proposition, but bear with me. We, who were born to consumerism, can scarcely fathom a life without our next purchase and our next pay check. We have ingrained in ourselves the habit of spending for our upkeep and our perks. Along with it comes the need to increasingly augment our earnings to sustain the process. Meals, entertainment, possessions, novelties and other delights all have an inherent monetary value. As a result, our lives have been, and continue to revolve around, making money to spend money. It's really most of what most of us do. We work ourselves to exhaustion, and then we reward ourselves for our hard work with trinkets, trips and nick-knacks. Is it not?

The inconvenient truth is that the sum of our contemporary code-of-ethics also boils down to economics and financial gain. We have, as a society, decided that our finances rule us, and thereby we guide our decisions and our actions almost exclusively by them. We let our hungry purses guide our conscience, and we have the folly of telling ourselves it's for our own benefit.

What's more, the progress of our society came at the cost of our humanity. By misrepresenting truly honourable banners – such as equality and mutual understanding – we have left behind time-honoured values that addressed the nobler side of human nature, and we substituted them for the cold practicality of material wealth. Ironically, materialism promotes nothing of equality and understanding.

Over the course of a couple of centuries since the Industrial Revolution, we increasingly told ourselves we were freeing Humanity from moral bondage, and then we have enslaved ourselves to our finances and our perks via consumerism, hedonism and decadent convenience. Whether we have been induced to this error by interested parties, or whether we have jointly arrived at this stage by our own choices is less relevant than the fact that we are here; though it would be an interesting sociological exercise to analyse this progress from an objective viewpoint.

Be that as it may, by our ethics of today, an individual is worth his NET worth as a consumer or investor. The individual is thence not a complete person in the pragmatic eyes of contemporary society, but merely a piece on the great game-board of macroeconomics. Human dignity is often reduced to legal formalities, media debates or the individual's ability to purchase it. Likewise, social relationships are very much interdependent with material wealth, and society in general rewards only financial success, and mainly when this is proven through the trappings of monetary triumph.

By this maxim, our perception of objects, people and standards become fluid. Merit is found not in *"being"*, but in *"owning"*. Always? No. Of course not. Fortunately, not. We are still at a transition, a crossroads. The change is incomplete, albeit we are at an advanced stage. A dangerous stage.

Our contemporary principles tell us individuals and organisations *"deserve"* as much as others are willing to pay them for the benefits they claim to offer through goods and services. What the thing is becomes less important than how the thing is presented. The objective becomes then to distort perception of these benefits so that others grow to be willing to pay more than the intrinsic value of that benefit.

The advertising community's codes of ethics notwithstanding, we are left with the impression that any great marketer's objective arguably lays there: To make something appear more than what it really is, in the eyes of the targeted buyers. How else can one explain a prêt-a-porter suit and a TV set reaching similar market pricing? Are there not much more logistics, employees, infrastructure, components and specialist craftsmanship into a TV set than into a set of clothes? How else can one explain the phenomenon of brand overvaluation, where similar products are dissimilarly valued by such vast margins? Differences in quality? Hardly. Qualitative differentiation is seldom the cause of overvaluation.

In marketing and advertising – and indeed in the free market – subjectivity reigns supreme over objectivity. While in our contemporary code of ethics this type of phenomenon is justified by the renewable material enrichment it causes, it is undeniably a distortion of perception that provokes ripples in the foundation of valuation and the fabric of our morals, the detrimental consequence of which is relativism and inconsequentiality. Yet aren't these same consequences instrumental to consumerism? If so, aren't they desirable? This is one of many dichotomies afflicting our contemporary global society.

In spite of our technological advancement, Global society has traded much of its progress for its soul. The higher aspirations that were once our own to cherish have been threaded upon by the soulless industry of self-gratification. In essence, we pursued quantity in growth at the expense of our quality as a people.

Though we have perhaps started on the right path, through distorted anthropocentric ideals we have ceased to empower our better side to surrender to our primeval instincts. We accepted that the search for pleasure and the sating of our cravings is within our DNA, and denied the other half. We decided to admit that our animal passions are indeed very powerful, and we have surrendered much of our spirit and intellect to sate them. We embraced the animal within and encased our conscience. We chose our convenience over our accountability.

Today, timeless institutions such as morality, marriage, fidelity, monogamy and family, have been deemed mere inopportune paradigms, and cast aside to make more room for hedonism and consumerism. However, in our present considerations, we, as a society, have forgotten that these institutions were not mere social conventions. They were indeed historical creations that enabled society to exist within communal parameters. They were instruments that came to exist, in order that we could curb our more destructive instincts and turn them into something better; a code that allowed us to live in relative harmony within a larger community.

Like these institutions, our contemporary society has forgone the habit of promoting certain moral values and certain codes of conduct that were once at the very heart of our social identity. That we were always and remain imperfect is less important than the will to pursue higher aspirations. In our search for comfort, we forgot that, and by our lack of memory we were diminished as a society.

We are choosing instead a pragmatic approach. We are choosing a code that is measurable and quantifiable: Material wealth. Yet the ethics of material wealth are excessively malleable and corruptible. They are prone to absolute pragmatism and relativistic values that are not constructive; just convenient. After all, if only wealth is rewarded, then what is there to stop us from doing anything and everything to achieve wealth?

By our very human nature, it is, in my experience, paramount that society promotes a higher moral code to serve as a light, by which the individual can guide his conduct in the valley of shadows that constitutes purely pragmatic thought. Law & legal punishment alone are insufficiently strong to promote ethical behaviour, for the unlawful expect to escape civil and penal penalties, and they are too often right in their assumption.

The impoverishment of our sense of community and the destitution of human dignity, associated with valorising the sole objective of financial supremacy over every other human accomplishment, generates a moral manipulability that is harmful both to the individual and to society as a whole.

This is our contemporary reality. This is the dilemma of an entire species – our species – with regards to its identity. Does it have to be like that? The answer is quite simply: No.

The search for something better is also in our nature. We all thirst for evolution. We all hunger for more than the world can give us. The search for the divine and the sublime is within our DNA, just as our animal urges are. They are there and they are strong. We can choose to feed on them. We can choose to foment them and to harbour them until it can eventually become our reality. As with most things, the ability to choose a better destiny is within our reach.

****

Chapter II

THE COLOUR OF DEMOCRATIC RELATIVISM

Legality is not always congruent with morality. I perceive this as fact. If you also have noticed this fact, then you may have tried to understand the mechanics of why that is.

Henry D. Thoreau – XIX century author, poet and philosopher – described the situation thus:

> *"Unjust laws exist; shall we be content to obey them, or shall we endeavor to amend them, and obey them until we have succeeded, or shall we transgress them at once? (...) A man has not everything to do but something; and because he cannot do everything, it is not necessary that he should do something wrong. (...) I do not care to trace the course of my dollar if I could, till it buys a man, or a musket to shoot one with, the dollar is innocent, but I am concerned to trace the effects of my allegiance (to the State). Must the citizen ever for a moment, or in the least degree, resign his conscience to the legislator? Why has every man a conscience, then?"*[i]

Henry Thoreau seems to propose that individual conscience must take precedence over legislation, which is in fact what he pursued in life, at personal expense. This makes sense in light of a representative democracy, where the individual is not directly connected to legislation, but rather acts through a third party: The elected representative.

Yet, morally speaking, if the law that is proposed and passed by legally elected officials stands in stark contrast to the moral conscience of the individual that elected them, to what extent is that individual morally accountable for it? To what extent is he bound by it? To what extent should he abide by it, when it stands against his values and his conscience? These are not easy questions to answer, if we think of them in a rule-of-law context.

Naturally, Thoreau was speaking of taxation when he wrote his text, but that is by no means the limit of its meaning. Legality is not always synonymous with ethics and moral values due to a great many motives.

An easy – albeit incomplete – way to put it is that legal systems the world over have been distorted, over time, to accommodate the financial interests and political aspirations of certain oligarchies and the groups supporting them. Wherever they indeed happen, demagogy, proselytism and the promise of wealth doubtlessly have the power to distort constitutions and articles of law. This is subconsciously clear to most of us. We perceive this both instinctively and by means of an educated mind.

Another factor of the incongruence between law and ethics is our inherent human fallibility. Whether deliberately or inadvertently, we are, as a species, susceptible to flawed decisions. Even when we are supremely well intentioned, our educated decisions are greatly dependent on the quality of the information either obtained by us or delivered to us. If data is insufficient or incorrect, we are induced into error.

We are also prone to self-preservation, and in that tendency, we are predisposed to formulating decisions that will not result in adversity for ourselves and those we protect. Some of us will only activate this characteristic when we feel threatened, but then again, the identification of a threat can be highly subjective.

Finally, all of these factors are conducive to corruption. Many of us are, after all, easily seduced by the perspective of personal gain, which may come in many forms including monetary gain. Those we place in the position to decide things on our behalf are no different and – either by nature or by demerit of their position – they are more regularly tempted than the average citizen. By their corruption, laws pass that should not come to pass. Legitimised by a democratic system – or imposed under totalitarianism – they endure. Yet we forget that government is a social convention. We forget that its legitimacy is permeable to society.

We are living a time of great hypocrisy. Truth is buried in a syrup of continually changing interests, of which the least consideration is the human dignity of the individual citizen. Whether under the boot of a dictator, or in the freedom proposed by today's imperfect democracies, this is a time when concepts and ideas are blatantly distorted, and half-truths are divulged, with the clear objective of dividing public opinion, and creating a popular mass supportive of the agendas of certain prevailing hegemonies.

Either irresponsibly or by design, information is frequently mishandled and deformed, to the point where even the obvious becomes questionable. In the Age of Information, we are more often than not greatly misinformed.

For instance, there are entire populations that erroneously believe that they are living in a true democracy. True democracies are in fact extremely rare. Think of it! In its purest ideal form, democracy needs to be a *direct democracy*, where the voting public is ideally composed of all adult citizens, who directly partake in the political and legislative decisions of their society. Such a system presupposes free access to accurate information[ii]. Where does that actually exist? How impractical would it be?

In most present-day democracies – parliamentary, presidential, constitutional – the voting public elects legislators and officials to represent them, using their best judgement. This happens either via direct vote or indirect vote, the latter being even less democratic than the former. These individuals would, ideally, have proven adequate qualifications and perfect access to information. However, this is still untrue of most contemporary democracies; even model ones. The voting public's best judgement is invariably clouded by poor education or political propaganda, and perfect access to reliable information is still deemed impractical, even among government officials. How can then a democracy be genuine if the truth behind facts remains hidden from the public, and even from civil servants? How can the choices made by the voting public and legislators and executive members of governments be democratic with so many secrets, and disinformation looming about them?

In my view, the only intrinsically admissible secrets to democracy should happen out of the concept of *"veil of ignorance"* as established by John Harsanyi[iii], and later explored by John Rawls[iv] for the principles of justice, as applied in Law. By this notion, politicians and legislators should, at all times, be kept ignorant of the relevance of new laws to their specific condition and social standing, so that they would take an impartial stance. It is a difficult concept to implement, but it would be one that could ethically justify secrecy and ignorance in government.

I sometimes have the impression that, at some point in history, it was realised politically that offering the illusion of choice was more convenient than suppressing the ability to choose, and more convenient also than the ability itself. It may have been deemed more effective and less confrontational to sway and educate the public, than it was to subdue the population. It then must've become clear that exerting control over public opinion was of paramount importance. If so, instituting controls over information and education would be more suitable to credibly spreading disinformation than pursuing outright oppression. If this is in any way true, I believe they who decided thus were correct.

A true democracy presupposes free access to information; yet I could say that there is no country in the entire planet that can afford to inform its entire population about the ins and outs of government policies and government spending and state decisions. State secrets and legal secrets and personal secrets are the reality of any government, any political body and any legal body. Whether or not you wish to unfold the subject into the transparent and ulterior motivations of such secrets, and the practical, moral and ethical implications to having them, the fact remains that the secrets exist.

Besides, a true democracy can only be achieved under true egalitarianism. Where in our world of today does everyone benefit from complete fairness and parity? Where are rights and responsibilities entirely the same for every citizen, regardless of station? Nowhere. I'm not even referring to a meritocratic system, but merely a working practical example of a nation, where there are no privileges and no socioeconomic barriers, and where opportunities are equivalent throughout society. We say we have it, but we are yet to build such a place of compassionate social harmony and equality.

As it turns out, true democracy seems either impractical or inconvenient to nations as we are today. Competition among countries and the selfish pursuits of each national economy, as well as those of public and private bodies within a nation, make it improbable – if not impossible – to achieve a selfless and completely democratic state. We can, at best, reach the semblance of democracy, and only under the most altruistic of governments serving the most watchful of populations. These simulations may indeed exist today.

The most common situation is one where, by the secrets and compromises necessary to the governing bodies, oligarchies and hegemonies – both foreign and domestic – exert influence to obtain favourable legislation to further their own objectives, whatever they may be. Ideally, this happens within the law. In practice it happens in many different ways.

Hence, under the pretence of democracy, many rules are instituted that we should not brook, and then, more often than not, they are justified as *"will of the people"* or *"for the benefit of the people"* and are then imposed and enforced, by means of the established powers we have built and allowed to be built, for regulation of our society.

The compromised viability of democracy might still be acceptable in the view of honourable citizens if its purpose was incorruptible and, when conditions allowed, a glimmer of true democracy could still surface. Alas, the reality is a tad different. We are each often left with the impression that, for every philanthropic governmental decision, there is an ulterior private interest lurking in the background. Is that always the case? Maybe not, but too often *"money"* and *"economy"* are shouted more loudly than *"public duty"* and *"public service"*.

Yes, national economies are still interdependent with private interests. Yes, for the general populace to have access to basic benefits someone must foot the bill. Yes, for our economic systems to exist private enterprises must be viable, but must they rule all of us so extensively? Must private interests supplant public ones? Must there be no limit to the insatiable appetite for profits? Must the wealth of corporations take precedence over moral values?

I say that if we do not impose a limit – a moral limit – to corporate and state greed, that limit will eventually manifest itself painfully and unavoidably to haunt us and our descendants.

Make no mistake: The intelligences involved in perpetrating the twisting of modern democracy are extensive and admirable in their competence. They don't confront. They seduce. They focus on making the general gender their ally in pursuing their own ends. They extend their tendrils into the values of our society, and slowly and constantly mutate them to suit their objectives. They co-opt the individual by formatting the masses with guile and with extravagance. They pursue their greed by fomenting hedonism. They perpetrate corruption with collusion. They offer *"candy"* laced with *"drugs"*.

Are we so easily deceived? Yes. Remember that we have an instinct toward self-satisfaction. It develops from self-preservation. It is relatively easy to tap into that aspect of our being to seduce at least most of us. In fact, if we don't conscientiously oppose this instinct, self-indulgence automatically becomes our path and inequity our destination. Only ethics holds us in check. So, by eroding our conscience with a substitution of moral values, it becomes easy to corrupt through self-gratification. This is how the seduction is perpetrated. Without a conscientious opposition, hedonism is Man's natural pursuit.

Seduction through self-gratification is a tool to manipulate the general populace. It is also essential for – and symbiotic with – any economy based on rampant capitalism – which we also identify as consumerism – for the latter propitiates the means, through which the hedonistic maxim becomes a viable and continual economic cycle, even if an arguably unsustainable one. This relationship is of paramount importance for some systems of government to function properly. We will approach this topic in greater detail in the next chapter.

For now, bear in mind that, in our rapidly changing society of today, it is possible to detect initiatives bent toward the modification of moral values; some informed and coordinated, others just existent. After many decades of a progressive erosion of traditional moral values, at the present stage, the concern for subtlety is diminished in these initiatives.

The banners of these movements range from the clamour for social justice to outright hatred for the conventional. In a sea of often conflicting notions and interests, the noble, the egocentric and the whimsical demand to be treated with equal dignity, regardless of the content of their demands. They all contest the validity of traditional values, at one aspect or another, to further their own agendas. Between minority movements, quirky new religions, anthropocentric extremism and fourth generation self-serving rebelliousness, society finds itself in a flux of ethical currents, the result of which is utter relativism.

Relativism is a school of thought that regards all points of view as being equally valid; thereby having only relative, subjective value. It is repulsive to the concept of *"Truth"* as an absolute fact, and it prefers to admit only context and perception.

Defenders of relativism claim that our own cognitive bias thwarts objective observation, as would collective cultural prejudices and favouritism, which we would allegedly be incapable of resisting. On the other hand, opposition to relativism is often rooted in the claim that there is no great social or moral gain in forsaking practical ideas such as social objectivity, normative consistency and absolute truth.

While the debate goes on in academic circles, in practical terms, relativism has been incorporated and accepted into the *"politically correct"* ethics of contemporary society. It is useful in settling politically inconvenient opposition, and it is a serviceable demagogic tool. If anything, relativism is certainly a means to enable the promotion of antagonistic ideals, without the necessity of incurring direct ethical inconsistency or confrontation. It is an inestimable political and propaganda tool. Yet how valid is relativism per se?

Let's start at why it takes root among the people. The great majority of the Human Race is concerned about being accepted socially. We desire the consonance of our peers. We want their approval. We want to belong. It is in our nature to desire social acceptance, and as a society we foment this natural characteristic even further.

The result is that most of us are also concerned about being right. Being right often also means that we will meet with general approval; hence the concern. We used to accept that for one person to be absolutely right, another had to be absolutely wrong, which indeed had a potential for generating discomfort.

Relativism claims to provide a way where two dissonant parties can be simultaneously correct whereby there can be no such discomfort. This is undeniably socially appealing. It bypasses any real necessity for proving a point, and it circumvents the need for any democratic process. It falsely generates the impression of social inclusion by proposing the impossibility of exclusion. Is that realistic?

It is folly to readily assume that two people defending diametrically opposite principles will truly both be correct. To me, this is more fantasy than fact. If I think "A" is not "B" and another thinks "A" is "B", how can we both be assumed to be correct? The only way we'd both be equal in our assertion is when we are both wrong; meaning both "A" & "B" are actually "C".

Even if not diametrically opposite, different conceptions on a same reality are hardly ever both equally correct. They may remain evenly applicable, but they are seldom truly equivalent. Normally, they are deemed correct while they are both hypothesis and then, once proof is produced, one is proven and another disproven. In other words, divergent views on truth are only both correct while truth itself remains undiscovered.

Sir Isaiah Berlin once expressed, purportedly in defence of relativism, that to *"confuse our own constructions with eternal laws or divine decrees is one of the most fatal delusions of men.[v]"* I daresay the affirmation speaks only of Man's admission of Man's limitations in identifying truth. Yet, once truth is identified, it must remain.

Just the same, as a theory, relativism deals only in *"opinions"* and totally precludes the existence of *"truth"*. It stands in stark contrast to absolutism. At its core is the denial of any absolute fact.

Much like utilitarianism strives to morally legitimise a desirable outcome via circumstance, relativism understands reality only in face of context. According to this principle, what is truth to one individual – or culture – may not be truth to another. This would falsely dictate that there is no one truth, but many *"truths"*. However, truth is by definition absolute. Therefore, what relativism denies is in fact the existence of the very concept of truth. It accepts only circumstance. It relishes in argument.

Does this begin to sound convenient? It may to someone who feels like an outcast because of their personal choices. It may to oligarchic powers pursuing socioeconomic hegemony. Nevertheless, when we accept that anything goes, as long as there is plausible justification, we must also remember that what goes around comes around. There are grim consequences to relativism.

One is the illusion of tolerance without the practical benefits of it. Contrary to popular belief, relativism does not promote social understanding. No. It simply proposes that you ignore other opinions, whilst accepting that they can co-exist, with equal status as your own. Is that understanding at all? Quite the contrary. What relativism proposes is an unfeasible society, where no one listens, and where no common ground can be achieved. It proposes apathy.

True tolerance is this: That I may have friends with different lifestyles, beliefs and divergent sexual orientation does not mean that I agree with them on all their choices. I may like the person, respect their choices and still disagree. Likewise, disagreeing with any stranger about their choices does not immediately mean that I nurture any resentment toward them. Is that such a difficult concept to understand?

Alas, we are sometimes suppressed in our will to accommodate different people and their beliefs by their own instantaneous antipathy to our variance of views. I have to say that among the most intolerant of interlocutors I have personally encountered, are those who demand tolerance from society for their divergent views. So much for democratic relativism.

In relativism, you don't listen, analyse and then either accept or deny an opinion. Instead, you just hear and acknowledge; after all there is no need to incorporate another's idea, so why scrutinise it? There is no need to prove right and wrong, good or bad if your opinion will be automatically approved as valid. Society then becomes prey to individual convenience and unilateral perspective, at which point it crumbles into disorder.

If a compromise between absolute truth and circumstance becomes inevitable, instead of pure relativism, I rather appreciate the views of John Rawls insofar as they pertain to a *"human innate sense of justice"*, and its relevance to moral judgment and moral motivation. The concepts of *"reflective equilibrium"* and *"considered judgments"* that arise from the sense of justice Rawls describes could indeed befit the flexible adequacy necessary to diverging points of view, in face of inconclusive fact.

Assuming there is no consensus on a central truth, and assuming that considered judgements are impressions based on qualified moral beliefs – however applicable – by the standard of reflective equilibrium, if two or more such judgments were to disagree in some way, due process should follow with an adjustment of the various beliefs until they are in *"equilibrium"*.

In other words, Rawls proposes that legal and moral divergences be settled at a mean, wherefore they could provide consistent practical guidance. He further makes the case that a set of moral beliefs in ideal reflective equilibrium equates to the underlying principles of the human sense of justice[vi]. Rawls also argues that entrant principles of justice cannot be justified, unless they are shown to be stable; meaning also impermeable to constant change.

In my view, this brings us back to the fact that, without truth – without absolute fact, or in its absence, a generally accepted replacement – there can be no effective moral and legal system to guide social conduct.

If *"what is true for you is true for you, and what is true for me is true for me,"* as the pre-Socratic Protagoras is reported saying, and its inverse *"what is true to you is not true to me,"* both apply, then no general rule applies. How sustainable is a society built on that premise? The answer is simple: It is as sustainable as the strongest party in it.

The foreseeable result of any relativistic society is inevitable conflict, at which point the strongest will prevail over the weakest. As multiple parties pursue their respective conveniences and objectives, in detriment of one another, and without a central conciliatory force to determine moral justification, the strongest party will emerge victorious. Isn't this obvious?

This is not new to mankind. Relativistic anarchy is indeed the oldest form of social order we've developed. It coincides exactly with the behaviour of wild animals, and perpetually changes to suit the convenience of the alpha male first, and then the pack. As you may have inferred already, it culminates in a dictatorship of the strongest. Historically, it evolved into absolute monarchy. The *"novel"* movement of relativism is in fact recreating the anarchism that heralds a dictatorship of the mightiest.

Shocking, isn't it? Relativism is supposed to be exceedingly democratic, yet it ends in absolutism. Ironically, many revolutionary movements of the past fought the form of government called *"hereditary absolute monarchy"*.

Serious and altruistic social movements, bent on the change of paradigms, have been historically proven as an important tool of society for the pursuit of equality. Still, while some resulted in positive social advancements, others resulted in decay. Invariably, they are corrupted at some point. Generally, greed and privilege are the forces behind corruption.

Sometimes movements – and their goals – are still worthy in spite of their corruption, but only when there is truth behind them. The Ionian school of philosophy, Confucianism, Christianity, Protestantism, the Industrial Revolution, the French Revolution, the Socialist Revolution and Consumerism are examples of different types of movements that promoted notable changes of paradigm, in traditional socioeconomic systems and codes of ethics. Like these remarkable movements, there were myriad others in the course of recorded history that either succeeded in leaving a mark that endured to-date, or were suppressed. Those that prevailed in some form or another did so based on the sustainability of an absolute truth behind them. Conversely, extinction of failed movements came about either through repression – violent or otherwise – or as a result of inborn inconsistency.

Inconsistency is a characteristic that is prominent in the democratic relativistic movements of our time. While there are certainly many serious and philanthropic movements, I find that a great number of organised lobbies are not more than short-term agendas for the furthering of largely undeserved privileges for certain segments of society. Relativism provides us with no criterion to tell them apart.

For example, it seems trendy in certain places and circles to criticise the more conservative standpoints of religions and traditional belief systems. Ignorantly, criticism comes toward religious dogma and religions' unswerving defence of points of faith. Where is the sense in that? Aren't religions all about the upholding of points of faith?

What's more, in the predominantly secular society of today, there are few – if not none at all – who can declare that they are forced to follow a religion against their conscience. If following a religious system is voluntary, then how can it be that a relativistic democratic society deems it necessary to admonish religious dogma?

By the chief principle of relativism, if you don't like something, you're supposed to let it be and simply not be a part of it. Leave it to those who adhere to it. Yet while most religions seem able to coexist with other convictions, relativists very inconsistently seem unable to do so.

Democracy and relativism should, by their very concepts, admit coexisting differences of belief, under a banner of mutual respect. Even legally the right to religion exists in many democratic countries and cultures. Hence, to democratic relativists, the existence of religious dogma should not be a problem. Then what is the real problem?

Some argue that the problem is that a religious majority influences public policy, in detriment of the opinions of the minorities. Above all in the model democracies of our time, majority rule suddenly becomes a serious inconvenience, but isn't that the pivotal principle of a democracy? Isn't that also the principle of utilitarian consequentialism at work? Again, valid but utterly inconsistent.

Be that as it may, I happen to agree that some basic rights and freedoms must be ensured even to minorities, even in detriment of a perfect democracy, so as to avoid a *"dictatorship of the masses"* and guarantee individual human rights. However, if this is to be so, it has to contemplate all minorities, and it cannot deprive the majority of its rights either.

Still, there are those intolerant few among minorities, who would not brook diverging opinions, even the opinions of the majority. They frequently use a discourse in defence of diversity and freedom, only as far as to impose their own secular dogmas over those of the religious. The inconsistency is evident.

There are some that go even further and say that many ills of our world are the direct result of religious dogma. They urge religions to become more democratic, which is conceptually ludicrous. Religions are not about public opinion or popularity. They are not businesses competing with one another for market share.

It is my understanding that religions, by their very proposition, are not democratic institutions. Instead, any serious religion claims to defend *the Truth*. Note that it is not "*a*" truth. Absolute truth, by definition, is unswerving and unyielding. There is no argument that changes an absolute truth. There is no change when socioeconomic and cultural context changes. As such, though they can adapt uses and customs, traditional religions cannot bow to fashion and convention in central dogmatic points of faith. Any church that would do it would be betraying its core beliefs and all its members.

Blinded by their own agendas, their own convictions and conveniences, those that attack religious dogmas relentlessly accuse religions of generating adverse social behaviour that results in adverse conditions affecting the entirety of society. Among common arguments to this end are criticisms regarding use of contraceptives and abortion.

Paradoxically, most religions that are contrary to contraceptive methods and abortion, as a means of managing a sexually active life, are also averse to the act itself when it is not associated to conjugal procreation. They tend to counsel against promiscuity and against profligacy for its own sake. Instead, they preach a life of self-control and fidelity to matrimonial vows. This is a completely consistent – and I daresay very responsible – standpoint.

For those who self-servingly hold that self-control is a statistical impossibility, and that contraception is the only answer, I submit that the largest populational concentrations on Earth happen in cultures that are not adherents to religious dogmas preventing use of contraceptives. In fact, the largest one is harboured in a socialist agnostic nation that systematically promoted abortion and sterilisation for several decades.

Still relating to the same example, it would seem to me that the problems associated with a solution, via use of contraceptives and abortion, are linked to a much greater extent to personal conduct outside the precepts of these religions than the following of them. So how can the blame fall upon religions?

The answer is indeed quite simple. People still instinctively want to be right. They want to be justified in their choices. They want the comfort of knowing they are with the majority of the herd. This is more important even when you chose something against your better judgement or against your moral conscience. Reaffirmation in face of error seems even more demanding than being correct in the first place.

Returning to the example of the controversy surrounding the theme of abortion, regardless of religion, it seems to me that there should be no controversy at all among people who understand the concept of personal accountability. Whatever the way you decide to look at it, the unborn child is always and in every way innocent. Yet, it is the innocent party that pays with its life for the folly of others. How can this be in any way morally justifiable? Where is the consistency?

The abnormal conditions argued in defence of abortion notwithstanding, an abortion performed to suppress a pregnancy resulting from a consented encounter – they appear to be the majority nowadays – can only be construed as a moral aberration. After all, it is the response of two supposedly responsible people to the foreseeable consequences of their acts. It can easily and very earnestly be described as one unborn infant paying with its life for the voluntary decisions of two biologically adult persons.

This is not religion speaking. It is pure Moral Philosophy. Think on it: Two people enjoy moments of carnal pleasure and then kill one infant in formation. I say *"kill"* without reserve because even a *"yet non-living fertilized blot of organic matter"* remains an infant in formation, if it was a viable blot. If it were an unviable one, the object of the controversy would be moot. So, two adults make a decision and impute dire consequences on a non-contributor third party. That is the objective fact. The rest is rationalisation and rhetoric.

This has little or nothing to do with religion. Religion being voluntary, it becomes a non-determining factor in the democratic equation of moral controversy in politics. The real problem in the controversy has to do with personal conscience, individual accountability, law, politics and democracy itself.

Here is the danger of indulging each and every banner without any reluctance or criterion. This is the peril of relativism. In the end, many of these movements do not exist under an honest and just cause. They merely suit the purpose of furthering the conveniences of a particular group, many times in detriment of the greater good. They very often fight not for a place under the sun, as much as *your* place under the sun; for the more radical the movement is the less malleable it is to prevailing opinions, and to the claims of other movements. So much for democratic relativism.

Historically, although I feel the changes in philosophical paradigms started all the way back at the Industrial Revolution, I identify the root of contemporary relativistic movements with the 1960's, when many social taboos were ruptured, in the advent of organised groups, and certain advancements in medical science.

Returning to our key example, I submit that the removal of practical consequences directly linked to acts deemed immoral, up until the discovery of the contraceptive pill, have enabled the pursuit of those acts with apparent impunity. This same impunity became the catalyst to a popularisation of immorality.

The rebelliousness of youth – using a new and very appealing social trend to affirm their independence before the previous generation – by and by took to the new practices. Then – having pursued licentiousness – when their offspring followed in their footsteps, they had no moral standing, with which to admonish the practice. Through repetition, what was deemed immoral became common practice; thereby being perceived as normal in the fullness of time.

Yet the change is still incomplete. There remain undeniable practical complications relevant to human nature in the *"normalised immorality."* Our change of demeanour has not changed our inbred emotional and physiological reactions. Emotional attachment and the physiological consequences associated with romantic involvement are still present. No matter how hard we try to turn our bodies into playgrounds, we are still human and we must learn to recognise that fact. Knowing ourselves, we must not forget how we have learned to restrain our more self-destructive urges and channel them productively. Moral codes, customs, institutions and religion surfaced as responses to this intrinsic human need. We set them aside at our own peril.

To those who argue the pill brought the promise of freedom and bliss, I say we have enjoyed over fifty years of what the hedonist and utilitarian currents have jointly proposed. Sexual freedom, anthropocentrism and ethical malleability have flourished and prospered all this time. Where is the incommensurable joy that should have resulted from it? Where is the humane brotherhood that would emerge to embrace a selfless existence of its own accord? It isn't here. Quite the contrary, we've become selfish and heartless in our petty pursuits, and pharmaceutical companies were the ones that prospered alongside abortion clinics.

The chief inconsistency of contemporary relativistic society is this: In all our relativism and democracy, it is inadmissible, in contemporary society, to cry out against what we perceive as a travesty of our traditional moral conduct. We must accept the *"politically correct"* in all its shapes and forms, and we may not defend the moral code that evolved, when we first realised that the unchecked indulgence of our animal urges brings disharmony to our midst. Those that dare are branded bigots.

Ask yourself: Who establishes the political policy of the *"politically correct"*? Look at the term and find the answer.

We are living a time of great hypocrisy. It is a time of ample freedom of information, and also a time when certified information is owned and controlled. It is a time when words have lost their meaning, and are instead misused frivolously to promote the disassembly of sophisticated traditional moral values, with the objective of rendering the popular mass more pliable to the conveniences of certain empowered oligarchies.

In a world where democracy is pervaded by political aspirations, fed by corporate interests, democracy empowers those who excel at consumption. It allows for the cries of those who are libertine and irresponsible because, having no other consolation in life, they soothe themselves with material wealth. In the name of the meek and the oppressed, contemporary democracy favours those who are instrumental to economies and forgets its docile constituents. It accepts the concepts that further the ulterior goals of those already empowered, and is deaf to the pleading of other interests, whatever their cause.

If society were to be truly tolerant and democratic, and if society were to be truly relativistic, then it would be impossible to deny voice to conservative currents that want to revive and safeguard time-honoured values, even if they were disputed. At the very least, it would be admissible that these older values should co-exist with new agendas; yet it is not so. So-called minority movements seem not contented in being acknowledged. They want their views to dictate policy affecting everyone. So much for the *"democratic"* side of democracies.

If democratic relativism were to be earnest in its purpose, dissonant voices – politically incorrect voices – should be heard. Yet they are branded, gagged and ridiculed; and then they are dismissed as quickly as they dare to cry out in defence of their ideals. Money speaks louder. Economy is supreme.

* * * * * * *

Chapter III

INSATIABILITY & GREED

Two misconceptions are widely propagated at present:

A. *"You have a right to be happy."*

B. *"Happiness can be owned."*

If you haven't realised the chief hypocrisy behind consumerism yet, try to analyse the promise and the actual result of consumerist relationships. Shall we start with the two premises above?

First and foremost: How is happiness a birth right? What legitimate right does anyone have to happiness when they come into existence? If we do nothing to deserve it, how is it that it can be due to us? How is this right to be delivered? This is folly.

It can be argued that, although we have not worked for our happiness at the time of our birth, our parents and ancestors may have done so on our behalf. Yet, while our parents may have deserved their happiness, and while that happiness may spill on us, as of the moment we are born, because of our parents' benevolence, we ourselves have no legitimate right to be happy until we work in some way toward achieving – or at the very least conserving – that happiness.

The United States Declaration of Independence puts it rather prudently thus: *"We hold these truths to be self-evident, that all men are created equal, that they are endowed by their Creator with certain unalienable Rights, that among these are Life, Liberty and the pursuit of Happiness.*" So, as Thomas Jefferson, Benjamin Franklin and their colleagues envisioned it in the XVIII century, the right pertains to the pursuit of happiness rather than happiness itself. To me, this makes more sense.

People certainly should have the opportunity to procure their happiness, but this is an objective. It is an ideal to be achieved through hard work and through a fair amount of applied wisdom. It is not something given. It is rather something to be earned.

We collectively seem to have forgotten that. Over the course of only a couple of generations, we very expediently allowed ourselves to be deceived by the concept that happiness will fall on our laps spontaneously. After all, we are citizens and we have a "*right*" to it. Where does it say that citizenship, even when allied to conscientious social responsibility, automatically entails a "*right*" to happiness? If there is such a legal text, it is much deceived.

It sometimes vexes me that, in many cultures, the concept of *civil rights* doesn't walk hand-in-hand with the concept of *civil duties*. People seem to just want to sit around and let the world present them with opportunity and fulfilment. This is utter rubbish. It used to be said onto children: "*You reap what you sow*". That remains true. If you sow nothing, what can you reap but by opportunism and thievery?

Secondly, how can you "*own*" happiness? How is happiness to be defined as something even tangible so as to be possessed? Is happiness as permanent as material ownership or is it as transitory as our satisfaction with that possession?

The truth is that while we all have the ability to feel happy, very few of us takes the time to analyse what it is that really causes that happiness. What's more, a great number of us confounds happiness with other feelings; holding it to be one and the same with sensations and situations that bring only ephemeral pleasure.

Besides, I do believe the concept of happiness is rather subjective and fleeting at that. Certainly, if *"happiness"* would be something material, it would be called *"contentment"* instead. In fact, I sense that this confusion often is the case. In truth, I feel that whereas material wealth can certainly contribute to one's state of happiness, it is by no means its definition. If it were, there would be no unhappy millionaires and no happy needy person. Yet there are.

Should we obstinately decide to define happiness as congruent and coincidental with contentment, we should still find it difficult to correlate it to the consumerist ideal, for the concept of contentment is averse to consumerism in almost every way.

Consumerism is often defined in economics as the model, where a continually escalating consumption of goods is perpetually gainful to the financial system on local, national and global terms. In a broader sense, consumerism is seen as a socioeconomic order rooted on the continual fostering of the desire to purchase goods and services in ever-increasing amounts.

The problem is, of course, in the *"ever increasing"* part of the equation. Per these two widely accepted and complementary definitions, consumerism could then be construed to be synonymous not with *"contentment"*, but with *"insatiability"*. After all, it needs to be continually increasing. Needless to say, insatiability stands in stark opposition to contentment. If we proceed to assume that contentment is either congruent or conducive to happiness, then we should assume that its absence would in effect hinder happiness.

Hereupon we ask ourselves: How is it then that consumerism promises happiness, can't deliver it, yet it seems to work?

If you concede that happiness is either synonymous or at least congruent with contentment, and that contentment cannot be perpetual, and also that contentment is based – at least partly – on personal pleasure, social acceptance and plenty, then consumerism can be redeemed in its promise, proportionately to the above-mentioned principles. Add to this basic human nature and the theories of Abraham Maslow[vii], Charles Darwin[viii], Burrhus Skinner[ix] and such others, and you will have most of the ingredients you need to come up with a successful model for consumerism.

Ephemeral bliss conceded via the thrill, the novelty and the immediate practical, personal and social benefits afforded by the acquisition of product – e.g., goods and services – would, at least in theory, be conducive to new such acquisitions. As it turns out, this is often true.

As soon as contentment recedes into dissatisfaction, the memory of pleasantness compels the individual to a new positive experience. Memory of a positive feeling indicates self-gratification, via consumption, as a means to attain it. The cycle repeats itself from time-to-time, whenever the individual procures a renewal to the state of satisfaction, which depending on the situation can be yearly, monthly, weekly, daily or even hourly. This, in turn, would renew an entire supply chain and indeed increment the economy within that supply chain. So you see, under the light of consumerism, the process even makes sense.

So, in effect, consumerism proposes happiness not through contentment, but through insatiability and the incessant attempt to quench it. It depends rather on the illusion of contentment for the generation of temporary satisfaction. Therefore, discontentment is utterly necessary to consumerism, and indeed marketers have come up with a great many ways of harnessing, and even artificially generating, it.[x]

Certainly, under this premise, the happiness and sustainability of the great majority of businesses – and the people employed by them – would only happen, in the long term, if contentment were never achieved. Insatiability, which is perpetual discontentment, is therefore desirable to consumerism; even though it claims to provide the opposite.

Here's the indignity of the progression: Strangely enough, when *"fostering the desire to purchase goods"*, the advocates and agents of consumerism seem to promote the idea that consumption will indeed bring contentment, satisfaction and pleasure; implicitly equating these to happiness.

While the argument of promotion of instant pleasure is relatively safe in its own enclosure, more often than not, a product, service or benefit is sold under the illusion that it will afford the quenching of voraciousness to promote contentment, and thereupon generate a state of continued happiness. If insatiability is the goal, how can that be a valid argument?

It is a valid argument only because the concept of happiness is still subjective, and because there is no universally formal definition. The objective idea of happiness – and its causes – seems not to be clear in the mind of most people. Nevertheless, the sales argument on more than a few products and services is fallacious in this very sense; most of all in all those durable products meant to be automatically superseded or outmoded within a relatively short time-frame. This is the concept of *"planned obsolescence"* which is one of the most obvious expressions of the fallaciousness of the idea of *"happiness through consumption of goods"*. That is a deceiving statement.

While this common practice could undeniably constitute a *"lie"* in the strictest sense of the word, it is regarded as a *"white lie"* insofar as it is part of the reigning economic system. It is tacitly assumed that a judicious adult will know how to separate truth from exaggeration using sound judgement. Whereas this is arguably a valid ethical standpoint at best, it endures despite the creation of watchful consumer protection organisations. The ethics of consumerism allow it, but is this really ethical?

Think on it: While the manufacturers and marketers of a product should know exactly what it does and what it does not, not every adult is technically apt to judge the suitability of every product, or the *"clear"* poetic licence present in advertising. This sometimes brings controversies, but it is mostly argued that an adult should be able to discern exaggerations from facts in advertising.

Those that want to avoid conflict altogether choose to talk about the product very little – or not at all – within their ads; talking instead of greener things they want to associate to brand and product. It must be said that it is not at all uncommon to relate products to characteristics that are not intrinsic to them. Using a sort of *"halo effect"*[xi] via association with popular public personalities, high-living, humanitarian causes, ecology and other ideals cherished at present, adverts frequently divert attention from a product's true characteristics to the qualities of things associated to them artificially. Here adults should indeed be able to pinpoint and separate what is product and what is just talk, though it is often not the case.

Equally, what can we say about advertising and products directed to children? Can methods such as the attribution of *"halo effects"* via merchandising be acceptable when directed to children? Can advertising to children be in any way moral?

We already know that advertising directed to children is highly effective. It has several advantages, as children are eager consumers, socially pliable ones, they more readily accept new products and are easier to indoctrinate; where indoctrination may even transfer the habit of consuming certain products into adulthood and into new generations. Conceptually it is perfect. Morally it is perfidious.

Here's why: Children are not deemed conscientious consumers. While there are unscrupulous marketers and businessmen who deny it, humankind also knows that *"selling"* to children is highly controversial, in that their frame of reference regarding *"true value"* and *"true need"* is still in a stage of formation. Besides, at least in theory, children should have no income of their own, and their decisions should be subject to parental scrutiny, so the sales arguments should be directed to parents, not their offspring. What's more, many of the dainties, snacks and other products directed to children are deemed unhealthy by medical consensus. Connecting these products to popular cartoon characters etc. to attract children is utterly harmful.

By all logic based on any scruples, children should never be targeted directly by commercial media. Yet, companies employ the media to tell children that they need not only new toys and unhealthy foods, but also mobile phones, credit cards and designer clothes. Without any criterion to judge their real needs, children fall prey to the urging of the media – and failing that – to peer pressure.

Where are parents to restrict this ruinous progression and impose family values? Why do parents indulge their children in these unhealthy and needless desires? They do so out of several psychological devices, not the least of which is a sense of guilt derived from chronic absence.

More and more, parents are called to pursue their professional careers, even in detriment of private time, even in detriment of quality time with their family and their children. As a result, many children display such behavioural patterns as to indicate that they feel abandoned, and the hard truth is that they are indeed left deprived of sufficient attention from their parents. Feeling powerless to overcome the pressures of the contemporary work environment – that will require more and more commitment, and will not admit a parent reducing hours to tend their offspring – and simultaneously feeling guilty for not being there for their children, parents overcompensate by gifting their needy offspring with trinkets and perks that the little ones bid of them.

Some social communication venues maliciously tap into those feelings, often teaching children how to manipulate their parents to get what they want. While some countries have banned the practice, it is still very common in many places. Why? Because the ethics of profit will allow it. Commercial interests are placed above the welfare of children – and consequently the future of society in general – in the hierarchy of consumerism. The ethics of consumerism consent to a great many *"sustainable white lies"* and inaccuracies, in order for the *"fostering of desires for goods and services"* to go on.

In fact, these biased inaccuracies are no-longer even a moral discomfort to most professionals, as their generation has already grown in this unethical framework. They are, after all, necessary to the economic model proposed by consumerism, they have become ethically acceptable, in order to foment economic growth. In ethical philosophy, I suppose this would constitute a good example of utilitarian pragmatism put to practice.

The exception must be made that there are still ethical venues in marketing and advertising. All is not perfidy and corruption in social communications. Yet, as time passes, I see a growing tendency of departure from ethical concepts.

There was a time when I regarded advertising as a mere tool of marketing, aimed at introducing a product to its target public. It was an ethical concept wherein a product could be candidly described and given an identity that would attract those who were truly interested in it. Naturally, it'd be painted in a favourable light, but respecting its true nature and purpose. A spot in the sun would be found for it, but one it truly deserved.

Be that as it may, more and more we witness products being presented, not as what they are and what they do, but as symbols of status anthropomorphised, as if they could bestow attributes to a person. Many advertising campaigns won't even speak of the product itself, but simply strive to associate it to an emotion or another abstract concept. Is that ethical? Only in the eyes of profiteers. To anyone of good sense, the practice reeks of behavioural manipulation to sell people things they don't really require. Some companies even say they are creating new solutions, when in reality they are generating new needs.

You doubt it? The shortest path between two points is a straight line, so think straight: If a product is indeed essential to your day-to-day affairs, would you not already know about it? After the product has been introduced, after you tested it and approved it, would you truly need convincing? You may indeed require persuasion, if there are two or more homogenous products providing very similar benefit, and competing in the same geographic market, but other than that, would all the marketing tools that today compete for our cognition be at all as important as they have become? Would the apparatus of advertising, branding, merchandising, market research and all of the artifices of the disciplines that sway public opinion be as essential as they are today? Of course not.

A hundred years ago, almost nothing of this was part of daily human experience. People relied far more on the recommendations of their immediate community than the adverts on billboards, magazines, point-of-sale, TV and internet. Fifty years ago, all this wasn't as necessary as it is today. Most of it was already there, mind you, but it wasn't indispensable. The same can be said of many of our household appliances and personal gadgetry.

Marketing professionals of today are indeed the minions of industry and the priests of consumerism. Theirs is the task of understanding markets and people and products so as to keep the flames of industry burning. Theirs is the task of fostering the ever-increasing desire to acquire and to own. They must identify needs, and if they would be good professionals, they should even help create new needs. Where a product is not genuinely needed, it must be associated to a real need. While there are many forms to reach that goal, this is most commonly achieved through the offer of pleasure and social ascendance.

People need fulfilment to be happy. They need to feel good about themselves. They need to be accepted. Whether truthful or not, under the premise of consumerism, it becomes necessary to advocate that the achievement of social ascendance and personal happiness happens through acquisition and ownership of products and services. In essence, these products and services are to provide contentment and pleasure to the individual that owns them, and through contentment a sense of joy. More importantly, they are symbols of who you are and who you want to be.

The alleged contentment can be a function of a pragmatic necessity or of the search for personal bliss, but in contemporary advertising argument it most often comes as a function of social acceptance. The product will make you be a *"desirable person"*. Silly as it may sound, this is a functional system.

Economically speaking, consumerism is brilliant. It really works. The only catch is in finding ways of fomenting continuous growth. To that end, marketers have become very clever when it comes to finding ways of making working devices be discarded, redressing products for different target publics and convincingly advertising them as solutions to needs you never even had. When the argument is a myth, it even makes the system work better toward the renewing purchases. You go for a solution to a need you never genuinely felt, and in time, you get jaded, it ceases to make sense, and then you go for your next mythical need in a continual search for satisfaction. You will never sate it. You will never be done. Brilliant.

Note here that we are not even talking about the sale of flawed, counterfeit or pirated items. No. We are still talking about the promotion of sales for original product, under the premise that they will suit the technical purpose for which they are designed. We are talking about trinkets of technology, durable goods in general, tokens of social belonging such as fashionable clothes, reputable cosmetics etc. Even in these markets and products, we are still dealing in half-truths and inaccuracies that seem acceptable to the ethics of profit.

Again, I say: Is marketing and advertising always this unscrupulous? Certainly not. Are all businesses being run outside fair practices? Of course not. Yet there is a growing tendency towards the clouding of judgement where ethics is concerned. More and more the craving for profits makes ethics more elastic than it should actually be. More and more the need for perpetual growth distorts the natural practical realities of market dynamics.

At each new bending of authenticity, and each new step away from objective truth involved in the *"white lies"* of consumer society, the mechanics of consumerism brings myriad deliberate and consequential new misrepresentations to the collective ethos. In a sea of corrupt semantics, reality is lost to fantasy and Humanity becomes entrapped in a maze of mirrors and shadows. The meaning of things as crucial to the established relationships as *happiness* and *contentment* becomes compromised, so that the promise of happiness, through material contentment, may appear to be fulfilled.

If you stop to analyse what *contentment* really means, you will find that the proposition itself has always been misleading. Contentment is often defined as *"the state of being satisfied or at ease."* To be satisfied is to be sated, the opposite of hungry or needy or wanting. It is to be endowed of all that you would want. If something is missing, then the individual would not be contented. Then it must follow that happiness through contentment is a state of being where an individual is pleased with what is already available.

So, how can an economic system based on the continual sale of products and services be perpetually renewable, if it provides contentment at any given point? It can't. For consumerism to work well, it ideally cannot provide contentment. Ever. It must continually generate needs and wants. It must keep unfulfilled the promise of happiness through material gratification.

This is not a particularly difficult goal. Why? Material wealth is not capable of supplying perennial contentment. Shocked? Don't be. I'm just saying that in due course, we all need more. Things either get old, depleted or we grow jaded of things and experiences, and move on to our next fix. This is who we are. That is why consumerism works so well.

If not consumerism, then what does provide perennial contentment? If material wealth, the goal of almost every individual in our contemporary society, is incapable of satisfying human nature, what does? That question is indeed at the very heart of the matter; for it is there that you will find the reason why traditional values are systematically being dismantled in our time.

Professional accomplishment is a great source of day-to-day satisfaction. I'm not talking about the financial reward that a profession may bring, as much as I am referring to the pride one may take from performing well. Loving what you do and doing it well can feed an individual with much contentment; regardless of whether financial gain is exacerbated by the community's recognition of your skill. Sadly, many people nowadays sacrifice a desirable career for another that would pay better, whereupon monetary gain becomes the main – if not the only - objective.

Similarly, a life of altruism and philanthropy also seems to be highly satisfying even if challenging. It also appears that altruism is relatively inexpensive and requires very little in terms of luxury. Reportedly, fostering apathy for egotistical pursuits in exchange for an endeavour to better a community or to improve the world seems like a Herculean task, but an extremely gratifying one. It has the potential of filling an entire lifetime of constant dedication, and it can result in the overturn of many an unfortunate soul. These are worthy activities and worthy objectives that find too little reward in our society of today.

Spiritual pursuits are generally deemed to be sources of perennial contentment. Human beings have an innate thirst for the divine that can only be quenched by the metaphysical nature of a spiritual life. You don't have to be religious to be a spiritually inclined person. Still, most religions seem to satisfy their practitioners, and many of them preach a life of detachment from material wealth. As such, they are enemies of consumerism, some even declared enemies. Religion and philanthropy many times walk hand-in-hand, so that there is ample opportunity for personal fulfilment. Why then is religion relegated to a place in the side-lines of contemporary secular society?

Study and personal academic achievement are also goals that provide lasting gratification, among other benefits for the individual and for society in general. Invention and discovery are often linked to these pursuits. They need not be intrinsically attached to a monetary goal. The mere sense of success one can obtain from self-improvement, recognition and new discovery is immensely satisfying. Nevertheless, it appears that schools and universities find more and more focus on turning education into a marketable product, even in detriment of its primary purpose.

More commonly, the nurturing of a family and the witnessing of growth and improvement in one's offspring is absolutely fulfilling. Granted there are always ups and downs, but the project of encouraging a strong family, and building a future generation is certainly work-intensive, but completely rewarding as a whole. Yet today we see people who are too busy to partake in this experience. Overworked parents who delegate the raising of their children to television, video-games, nannies, teachers and other caretakers are more and more common, after all it frequently takes at least two adults to support a household at our present standards. There is so much we have come to *"need"* and competition is so steep that few today can afford to be outside the workforce.

To our discredit as human beings, at present, we seem to connect every aspect of personal accomplishment to monetary gain. As a society, we've taken the limelight off these other goals, and we've sacrificed much of their meaning in so doing. It became commonplace for people to give up their passions and their gifts for more lucrative professions.

Success has a value attached to it. Acceptance has a price. We make money to spend money.

Is that all there is? If so, I'm stricken with the sense that we will all be leading very empty lives, and we will not find true happiness. Indeed, I see many unhappy people around me, who are endowed with fashionable clothes, the latest smartphones and very auspicious careers. Don't you? One must hope that there is more than that. So why do we surrender to it?

The truth is that most of Humanity feels a need to be accepted socially. We want to belong in the herd and the herd foments this in us so that we will abide by the rule of the majority. If we want something that is against the rules of the herd, we want that rule to change. We will be admonished by the herd otherwise.

Hence, we must try to sway the herd, so that most members will come to agree with us. In that manner, we can pursue our convictions with the approval of society, and we won't be forced to opt between one and the other.

Here's the rub. That is why we are perpetually drawn into arguing about what is right and what is wrong. This is the heart of moral ethics, even if not its soul. We argue and argue our divergent points until we are all blue in the face because, at the end of the day, we want people to accept us as we are.

Consumerism proposes a way out. It proposes that belonging be attached to social trappings. You will belong if you dress in a certain fashion, if you carry with you a series of gadgets and symbols of who you are, and if you go to the places and do the things that will paint a readily recognisable picture of who you are, then you will be accepted. Your choice of neighbourhood, your choice of car, your attire, the hobbies you contemplate and other such things will tell other people who you are; or who you would like to be.

Does this way out propose a truthful and sustainable means of social inclusion? Is it coherent with human nature and will it really settle the matter of our differences? I don't think so. This is consumerism's proposal merely because it is instrumental to consumerism's goals. Nothing else. Many times, brands are not what they claim to be. Products are not what they claim to be. Likewise, people are not what they own. The mask almost never depicts its wearer.

I can own the same model car and live in the same neighbourhood and frequent the same restaurants that my neighbour does, and still we are different people, with diverse backgrounds and values and beliefs. Circumstance and ownership will not make us equal or even equivalent. I can be a bandit and he can be a hardworking man, and we can both have the same income and own the same trinkets. Contemporary society tends to afford us the same dignity based on appearances alone, but behind the smokescreen the hard fact is that the *"suit does not make the man"*.

Before consumerism, from ancient times, and until not so long ago, similar notions on worth based on wealth and position already existed. Even so, they were reserved for a select few. Most others had to search for ways of belonging that were far more demanding than material ownership, and required a lot more sacrifices and dedication. Before the rise of consumerism as the socioeconomic maxim, people in general sought social acceptance via their values and their actions.

By your deeds, people knew your worth. It was not your NET worth that mattered as much as your worth as a human being capable of relating to another human being, or a person capable of positively contributing to the community.

In this scenario, personal achievement is key if you want social ascension. Behaviour is of paramount importance if you want social approval. You are who you make yourself to be, not by what you purchase, but by what you do and the choices you make. If you want respect, you must bear yourself in a manner to produce that response in other people. It is more difficult, but it is a more honest way of relating to one another. It also seems to result in more rewarding and perpetual relationships, without as many negative surprises.

Fortunately, our society has not departed completely from this idea. There are still important factors of social behaviour integrating our present code of conduct that have endured from the previous model. Yet we are, by and by, corrupting these resilient notions, and we are replacing them with consumerist ideals, such as moral justification through success, and social inclusion via ownership of goods.

Needless to say, this is not ideal. It suits the people selling the goods better than it suits the people buying them. It would be best to reinforce the idea that people are not the sum of their belongings, but more so of their conduct.

At this point I feel it is necessary to clarify that I don't deem material wealth as an evil thing per se. Certainly people are entitled to own things that please them in some manner or another, or things that they feel they need to own for practical purposes. There is absolutely nothing wrong with that. However, placing one's focus and objectives solely – or even principally – on material ownership is folly.

People are much more than what they own materially, and if we set aside the paradigm of material wealth, we find that even the lowliest person gains dignity and pride in the things that are within their reach. Where the dynamics of human relationships are concerned, I feel that personal growth through contributions to family and community, professional pride, spiritual pursuits and other such things can substitute, with gain, the paradigm of social inclusion through material wealth, for they are all conducive to nobler acts than the pursuit of monetary profit for its own sake;

especially when that objective is pursued under the "at any cost" tenet.

It isn't even debatable that the quality of a person can be determined outside material wealth, for it has already been done. The problem is that a method that does not generate a sale is highly inconvenient to the economic model we have chosen for ourselves. What's more, it may contribute to our finding happiness outside material ownership.

How can that be possible? How can I be happy if not through material contentment? Dangerous questions indeed.

Well, if deeds become more relevant than goods in determining a person's social status, happiness could be construed to be found not in *"material contentment"*, but in *"personal fulfilment"* instead. Under this scenario, intellectual, social and spiritual fulfilment all become far more important than the perpetual accumulation of goods and the constant renewal of our collections of trinkets. This would indeed be disastrous to consumerism, though not quite so to capitalism in general.

This is why there remains such a strong movement toward changing the precepts of traditional moral values. In order to exist, in order to continue to grow rapidly, consumer society must replace the more sophisticated moral ethics that evolved out of the history of humankind with another more basic set. It must do so in order to foster and foment ever-increasing consumption of goods and services, even after our needs are fulfilled far beyond our basic uses.

Consumerism is impatient about growth. It is not enough to wait for the next meal-time, or for when your car is used-out beyond repair. Consumerism must make you hungry in between meals and make cars that are obsolete before they break-down. It is not enough to wait until renewal is actually necessary. New purchases have to happen more expeditiously than that. The aphorism is: *"If you're not growing, you're dying."*

For this reason, where a social value represents evolved moral ethics capable of providing lasting fulfilment to the human person, there is exactly where consumerism must dismantle and replace that value. It is a matter of survival. Perennial fulfilment found in fostering things such as a strong family, communal living, spirituality, harmony with nature and a principle of austerity must be replaced. They are values independent from monetary gain, and as such they represent a danger to rampant capitalism. Only in empty and ephemeral pleasures can consumerism thrive and reach its potential. Ideally, *"happiness"* must evaporate not long after it has been purchased.

How can the latest electronic gadgetry be marketed to a man that is content to have a functional obsolete version as long as it works? How can you tell a man who puts his priority in educating his offspring that he should renovate a perfectly functional wardrobe just to be fashionable? How can you convince a fervently religious man that the money he spends on charity would be better spent on a trip to a choice resort? How can the brand of a tennis-shoe achieve disproportionate value in the perception of a consumer, who is more confident in their personal worthiness? The blunt answer to all these questions is: *"You can't"*. Not unless you force the issue.

The logic of consumerism doesn't stand when faced with the evidence of true fulfilment, as promoted by adherence to higher values. Ephemeral contentment crumbles quickly, and every time it does it reinforces the need for something greater and more lasting.

Anyone who has a clear perception of what truly contributes for their happiness and what doesn't really matter is less permeable to the lures of consumerism. Such people are not permanent consumers as much as they are eventual buyers, and when they do purchase a product, they do it conscientiously so that they can obtain palpable and unequivocal benefits. This is perfectly adequate to capitalism, but palpably insufficient for consumerism.

People who don't easily discard their purchases for idle substitution are inconvenient to marketing men and to the advancement of constantly growing profit margins. Likewise, institutions that preach against the mindless accumulation of material wealth, or the impropriety of hedonism must be – and indeed are – marginalised by oligarchic interests, so that the hegemony of consumerism can be promoted. Unfortunately, this is done at great social cost.

Then again, this is hardly a difficult task. As we have already discussed, the individual is more often than not willing to give up value for benefit; even if it is timeless value for transient benefit. We intimately want a justification for abandoning higher purpose, in exchange for immediate pleasure. Nevertheless, knowing it is intrinsically wrong, once we start down that path, we want others to do it too; so that we feel supported and not guilty about it. That is the framework of our mind, and in the ethics of profitability, you would be correct to pursue this. Nonetheless there is that within that cries out and makes us uncomfortable about it. Something nagging in the back of our minds pricks at our conscience.

The inherent thirst for true happiness and fulfilment is within us all. It is regrettable, however, that we have allowed our society to shift this pursuit from greater objectives into petty ones. We should swing back. We should promote and valorise altruism and philanthropy, and we should admonish selfishness and idle profligacy, as we once did. We should endorse honour, valour, modesty and general goodness, and we should shun greed, ambition, vanity and common selfishness. At the end of the day, if we want to uphold the person, we must first undress that human being of all that hampers a clear view to them. Only then will we be looking at the person, and not their mask.

Yet consumerism works. Works for whom? It works most of all for the people selling the products, for they are content in their success. They witness their companies growing in size, NET worth and influence. They see their legacy being established. It works for the greedy and the needy in political and social spheres, for they achieve their goals through the instruments set forth by consumerism. It works for the unworthy and the wicked, for they can mask themselves very well under the golden lining of material wealth.

Is material wealth a moral sin? No; especially if you worked for it. Are all commercial relationships tainted? Of course not. Are all initiatives to foster consumption of products dishonest? Naturally not. Nevertheless, there is a growing tendency toward unscrupulousness as markets become more and more competitive, and profit margins become more and more scarce in face of competition. This is what we must watch. This is the danger lurking behind the smiling car salesman that is consumerism.

****

Chapter IV

THE ETHICS OF PROFIT

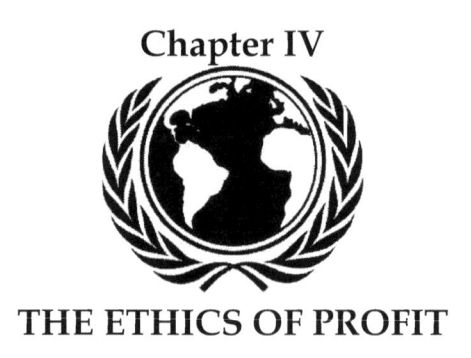

The word "ethics" has Greek roots in the word "*ethika*" and "*ethikos*" that meant "custom" to the ancient Greeks, which itself is related to the word "ethos" meaning "character". It is the broad equivalent of the Latin word "*mores*" from which the English word "morals" derives, though not quite synonymous, just as morals and ethics are not quite synonymous.

We all tend to think of the word ethics in the normative sense, as something meaning a set of rules and restrictions – things we shouldn't do – rather than a proactive term. That is not quite accurate. Law is the thing that proposes a set of restrictive "don't do's". Even though a few restrictions must occur for the didactics of ethics to work, morals and ethics are concepts more concerned with proposing "things to do" in order to obtain a harmonious social relationship to your neighbours and fellow citizens.

Take the word "etiquette". It is also derived from this concept, as a diminutive of the greater "ethics", to mean the "little things" we should do whilst behaving socially. Likewise, the concept of ethics – most of all Virtue Ethics – proposes a set of examples that we should follow in order to achieve a harmonious social order.

All of these concepts fall into place with the fact that human beings are subconsciously – and quite naturally –

made for living in society. The concept of "mirror neurons" – as initially uncovered by Giacomo Rizzolatti, Giuseppe Di Pellegrino, Luciano Fadiga, Leonardo Fogassi, and Vittorio Gallese at the University of Parma, Italy, in the 1980s and 1990s – attests to the fact that, unlike previous notions, we are designed primarily not for utilitarianism, aggression and self-interest, but for sociability, attachment and affection[xii]. We are intended for empathy. It is therefore in our nature to try to be a society; behaving and living in similar fashion, wanting to be included and accepted, desiring to share our existence.

While this is an auspicious prospect, it has its inherent dangers. If we are designed to imitate one another, and if we are designed to sympathise and acquiesce, what happens when the examples fomented by society are not quite the stuff of virtue? What happens when the interests and ideologies of governments and oligarchies supplant the ethos of an empathic civil society? Would it explain phenomena such as the appearance of militaristic societies, crowd behaviour, religious and patriotic fanaticism? Certainly.

It is hardly news at this day and age that we have more and more been divorcing traditional values, and replacing them with little more than materialism and consumerism. We more and more applaud and uphold values that were at one time frowned upon. Why? Who are we mimicking? Where will it take us?

With the continual migration from the cherishing of virtue to the valorisation of possession, as a mark of social inclusion, we are placing the fabric of society at a great risk. To put it plainly: If ethics are "things to do" and if materialism has become the main objective of individuals in our society, then the "Ethics of Profit" translates into everything one should do to achieve the sole objective of materialism, even in detriment of other values and objectives. This is a fearsome prospect.

The advantages to cash flow and the overall gains to economies notwithstanding, by allowing ourselves to be lured into the overvaluation of material wealth, and by deeming financial success as an acceptable justification for the absence of scruples, we are in essence eroding the very viability of the existence of commerce between communities. In fact, we may be risking the viability of the social communities themselves.

By bending our moral and ethical heritage to befit the need for continual betterment of our material capital, individuals, institutions and organisations have begun a chain reaction that has sent ripples into every plane of our Global society, for we are presently connected for better and for worse.

Let's take one very practical and relatively common example: A national company that manufactures overseas to gain competitiveness. If you are a company of local capital, and if your primary market is your own nation, why would you seek to establish manufacturing facilities abroad? Won't it cost you extra because of transportation and taxation costs? No. In fact it may well be the case that it won't.

None of us has to think very hard on it to find a handful of justifications to expatriate a company's industrial production; especially if we are placing profitability above other values. Cheaper labour forces, more affordable infrastructure, lower taxation and other such factors – including even what could be construed as slavery at your homeland – are financially justifiable factors, even in face of extra logistics costs and import taxes.

Whereas laws and moral values at your homeland would prevent a company from partaking in certain practices, there are places where such laws and ethics are bendable, or even non-existent. Hypocritical as it may sound, many corporations surrender to this type of situation. Why? Because consumers don't care to make it their business to know why a product made abroad is cheaper than one made at home. Because companies don't care to use people and resources to increase profits. Yes, it is cold and horrible. It is also morally inconsistent.

Make no mistake: Our present economic model has inherent flaws, in it that will mean the degradation of human dignity if left unchecked. The unrestrained pursuit of profits is ultimately conducive to unethical behaviour, for contrary to popular belief, no person truly has limitless appetites and no healthy economy can bear to grow constantly and perpetually, at ever increasing rates, without incurring into important social distortions, and without generating environmental impact.

That a company can grow speedily and steeply from time to time does not mean that it must – or that it even should – keep up that pace forevermore. It is perfectly possible and fundamentally viable to have periods of growth, stabilisation and even retraction, without any of these meaning a guarantee of perpetual success or certain downfall. The same seems not only true of national economies, but intrinsically healthy. The elasticity of economies propitiates opportunities for reinvention, and as a result, for the entry of new, innovative and small businesses and business models.

Stable markets are not necessarily stagnant. Shrinking markets are not necessarily dead ones. However, a market that is in perpetual growth is indeed doomed to break down at the apex. We have witnessed this phenomenon repeating itself in history. We have seen it recently.

For instance, in the XX century, the Great Depression of 1929 is very often studied as an example of how far the global economy can decline, but there are more recent equivalent examples such as the Subprime Mortgage Crisis of 2008 and the ongoing 2011~2012 crisis of the Euro Zone in Europe.

Whereas we should acknowledge that the repercussions of the events that respectively culminated in the Great Depression of 1929 and the Global Economic Crisis of 2008 have been largely different, so must the similarities in the causes of each crisis and their ethical implications be recognised. More to the point, though they are not exactly the same in nature and repercussions, there are important coincidences in the triggers of both crises, which should prompt the study of these crises not only in the light of elucidating the decline of economies, but more importantly in the study of the decline of moral ethics in societies where profit is the maximum goal.

It seems to me that there were ingenious socioeconomic mechanisms that came into play since the crisis in the 1930's to prevent the ramifications of a generalised financial bust, but there were none to prevent the cause effects of such a bust. Indeed, it appears that there were far fewer impediments to the financial crisis of 2008 than there were in the late 1920's.

In my understanding, despite being nearly eighty years apart, both world-spanning economic events share the same inherently (un)ethical causes. For starters, both events originated in the United States – meaning merely that they shared the same cultural basis – and both crises were birthed within the community of financial institutions, where it can be argued that profiteering reaches its maximum expressions. After all, modern banks and other financial institutions provide inherently intangible products, as opposed to tangible goods, and they depend on the productive activities of others to procure their own non-productive monetary advancement.

Moreover, a sense that the money markets were essentially deregulated – or largely left to self-regulation – in both scenarios allows for the impression that the state itself felt that the short and mid-term results were desirable. On balance, apparent affluence was that result. This meant that there were more people happy about the prosperity of the economy than people unhappy with it. The magic of *"pixie money"* created via clever accounting and financial devices seemed to provide unprecedented richness that even the lower echelons of society could attain. In both cases, the state then continued with deregulation with the objective of furthering a general sense of contentment, by allowing for the maximisation of profits, via a market free of government intervention. This is apparently beneficial, but what about fact?

In both cases, the promise of easy money via guaranteed dividends was conveyed, in order that capital could be harnessed from private sources. Meanwhile, within the financial institutions themselves, competition and the attempt at maximisation via clever accounting – sometimes inclusive of outright fraud – proved disastrous.

Pressure for continually improving results – both from investors and from the headship of financial institutions – would in due course enable an untenable scenario. Consequently, both the crisis of 1929 and its more recent counterparts were initiated principally by irresponsible – arguably unscrupulous – higher-risk stock market products and generalised lower lending standards.

That these high-risk strategies were very likely designed to attract investors, in order to meet growth quotas imputed to operators, by managerial personnel, is hardly arguable. The real question is how deliberately dangerous they were. Where banks and stock brokers unaware of the repercussions of their products? If so, did they not care to predict the potential for breakdown, or did they acknowledge and accept the risks with or without measuring them?

I can scarcely believe that the economists, engineers and mathematicians employed by these institutions were incapable of predicting the limits of the system they were commercialising, or unaware of the likelihood of a breakdown. I don't see incompetence as the mark of banks.

Rather I believe that, in both cases, the policy was clearly rooted in the desire for rapid enrichment, regardless of the long-term consequences, or perhaps trusting in robust governmental assistance. It deliberately ignored the long-term impracticality of the level of risk incurred, in benefit of short and mid-term profitability, in which case the policy was exceedingly successful both in 1929 and in more recent events.

That there could be, would be, and indeed were grievous repercussions to the entire global economy was not a moral deterrent. Under the ethics of profiteers, this is not their affair. Where profits are the supreme value reigning over every other premise, financial success is the redeemer of every evil.

That in both the crisis of the 1930's and in its more contemporary equivalent the collapse resulted largely from endemic fraud seems to pass unnoticed. That deliberate deceit seems to have flourished either unseen or unchecked is disturbing, for the illusion of affluence seems to suffice for the general gender and the state alike. No one asks where the money comes from, as long as it keeps coming.

This is, of course, mere speculation. Yet, I submit that it is self-evident that, where maximisation of profits is concerned, a self-regulatory system is inherently flawed. The profiteer cannot be expected to voluntarily respect a limit to his profits any more than mice would be expected to refuse cheese, or foxes would be charged with the safekeeping of a henhouse.

An illustration to this affirmation is found in the case of one Bernard Madoff, formerly the non-executive chairman of the *NASDAQ* stock market and founder of the Wall Street firm *Bernard L. Madoff Investment Securities LLC.* After his arrest in

December 2008, Mr. Madoff pleaded guilty to no less than eleven federal charges, and admitted to having perpetrated a massive Ponzi scheme that defrauded thousands of investors of billions of dollars. How was he able to maintain a fraud scheme worth more than sixty-five billion dollars secret for over a decade?

Though not invented by Charles Ponzi, the fraudulent system is named after him, who in the 1920's also notoriously perpetrated such a scam. The system consists of a fraudulent investment operation that pays dividends to its investors from capital acquired from subsequent investors, instead of utilising profits earned with the investments. Soliciting of capital is normally obtained with the promise of abnormally advantageous returns, the maintenance of which requires an ever-increasing cash-flow from new investors. The system is invariably destined to collapse because the earnings, if any, are less than the payments to investors. Madoff's scheme allegedly lasted over twenty years, and suspicions remain about the involvement of important corporations and institutions.

There can be no doubt that there were others involved in Madoff's scheme apart from his immediate cohorts. It is highly unlikely that all of his investors, collaborators and his partners – many of which certainly had a basis in finances and in economics – would not detect any implausibility in the alleged returns. I suppose blindness can be self-inflicted.

Be that as it may, until all of this came to light, in view of a manifest economic crisis, Madoff's firm was regarded as one of the topmost businesses on Wall Street. Until a crisis was apparent and the majority of investors became utterly discontented, Madoff remained free to embezzle and defraud. His clients did not feel compelled to ask how he was able to offer such promises. Blinded by greed, they did not care. Neither did the authorities scrutinise him, though it is arguable that they could have found cause for it. Why should they? Everybody was happy, weren't they? Exacerbated profits in the stock markets were the rule, weren't they?

Alas, Madoff's case was not an isolated event. Reports of suspicious activity on financial crimes seem to have grown twenty times between 1995 and 2005, and then doubled again between 2005 and 2009. Was all this completely unmonitored? No. As early in the roots of the latest crisis as 2004, according to the Federal Bureau of Investigation, there existed an *"epidemic"* in mortgage fraud in the United States. This was reportedly a significant risk concerning sub-prime credit. It appears lenders maliciously and consistently enabled loans that borrowers could not afford, which in turn would result in substantial losses to investors in mortgage securities. Indeed, in 2011, the Financial Crisis Inquiry Commission reported that mortgage fraud prospered in a propitious negligent environment[xiii].

With consequences that include the use of government funds to bail out private banks, the collapse of important financial institutions and significant downturns in stock markets around the world, the financial crisis of the first decade of the 2000's is not only a landmark in loss of confidence in the economy, it is also regarded by several economists as the worst financial crisis since the Great Depression of the 1930s[xiv].

Yet the United States government, though also grievously impacted by the consequences of the crisis, did not seem to be as concerned when the FBI presented its apprehensions back in 2004. Could it be that a blind eye was turned? If so, why? Was it because it was politically interesting to that administration to maintain the semblance of economic affluence? That is likely. It could also be a more nefarious plot.

If you consider that government agencies had palpable knowledge that fraudulent schemes existed – as evidenced – and if you consider that the ripples of the Subprime Crisis were felt with much more devastating effects in China and the European Union than at "ground-zero", it becomes plausible to imagine that the Subprime Crisis could have been allowed to happen, as a calculated risk to provide a non-violent deterrent to both EU and Chinese economic encroachment.

Granted this sounds farfetched, as such a plan would have been utterly irresponsible in terms, at least, of the human cost. Nonetheless a case could be construed to that effect, in view of the bail-out policies that the US administration pursued at that time, in detriment of reparations to the indignant population, and aimed at aiding the very same financial institutions that had partaken in the causation of the crisis. This, alongside the wars in the Middle East and Asia, which seem to have a greater bearing in the supply of petrol and gas to the EU, Russia and China than to the US itself, seem to fit the theory.

Again, this does seem farfetched and there were more flagrant and proven effects erupting from the Subprime Crisis. Wider direct results include numerous evictions and foreclosures in the housing markets, the failure of key businesses, prolonged unemployment, and consequential declines in consumer wealth corresponding to severe global recession starting in 2008[xv]. The fact remains that the recession impacted the Euro Zone and China with even greater relevance than the national economy at "ground-zero". This is, as they say, history. It is fact.

What also appears to be fact is that the moral values of our society have undergone palpable change. As proven by the governments that bailed out banks involved in the causation of the crisis, we are no longer morally bound to the consequences of our acts. We are indeed a society of conveniences and fluid values. We are a society of egotists. We don't mind any dismay we may cause as long as we get away clean. We don't mind reprehensible behaviour insofar as it provides returns upon investment. Unscrupulousness seems acceptable, insofar as it provides profits.

The ethics of profit envision only profit itself. According to this maxim, and contrary to the views of Henry Thoreau, as we have seen them, the implications and uses of the resources ceded by an investor to third parties are not the responsibility of the investor. As sociologist Zygmunt Bauman[xvi] already asserted, under this code, the investor is morally free from the onus of the misuse of his funds by the corporations he chooses to grace. Likewise, he feels morally free from the effects of his withdrawing financial support, as he envisions only the monetary relationship and has no direct concern with the operations themselves, whatever they may be. More often than not, the investor is remotely located and has no physical or emotional attachment to the operation he finances, their employees and the surrounding community. Similarly, we seem to no-longer feel connected to the consequences that befall the world surrounding us. Ours is only the concern for ourselves.

What this generates is utter impersonality and utilitarianism. People and organisations become but the means to an end. The objectiveness of the relationships solely based on profits leads to a perverse lack of moral imputations where the outcome is concerned. There exists complete dissociation between the power to pursue a course and the moral responsibility over the direct and the collateral effects of that pursuit.

Everything is reduced to numbers on a computer screen. Like the characters in videogames, these numbers represent real people and places, but the players sitting before the screen will have no moral restraint as to how they use the people and the places to achieve their gaming ends, as the results are immaterial to them beyond their private gain.

This is an entirely inconsequential relationship, but it becomes relevant when transported to the consequential practical results that the individual faces when society around him crumbles. Such utilitarianism, applied to people and places, may be instrumental to businesses but is also utterly detrimental to society. Similarly, the flexing of traditional moral values that is inherently necessary to achieve the ethos of supreme profits will eventually lead to social disintegration.

Given its successful instances, the amoral ethos of supremacy of profits overflows from business to business and market to market and even into interpersonal relationships. Eventually the novel ethos becomes the norm, and then it invites the increase of profits, at the price of a swelling in suspicion and animosity, both in the business environment and at a personal level.

If not intolerable solely for its moral implications, the compromise is wholly unacceptable in that it will eventually limit profit itself. Generalised immorality in business must culminate with a universal feeling of insecurity and adversity, and then with the imposition of restraints and greater scrutiny in all commercial relationships.

In other words, if most business and personal promises are not fulfilled, if dishonesty and exploitation become the norm, then there will unavoidably be a crisis in commercial and personal credit; the result of which is a socioeconomic collapse. If taken to its ultimate consequence, lack of confidence will cause commercial relationships to necessarily recede to payment upon delivery, via cash at sight terms, where cash may not even be a monetary symbol such as currency, but something even more tangible.

This is already becoming somewhat present in contemporary business relationships. More and more there are frequent misuses of credit facilities resulting in insolvency and in subsequent lack of confidence. It is likely also very palpable in personal relationships, though I am not qualified to judge it. As fair business practices are sacrificed for greater profits, the business environment becomes riskier and riskier, and the availability of credit seems to evaporate more and more, as profit margins are conquered with subterfuge.

In light of greater realisation of the impacts that rampant capitalism has on the natural environment and on the social environment, I submit that it is no longer conceivable that no limit is imputed to profits.

Even under the premise that continual profits are desirable to enterprises – and to world economy in general – we must at some point agree to deter the growth of profits. At the very least, it becomes painfully necessary to admit that we should deter profit at the limit of the mathematically feasible and the internationally legal, where law cannot bend to the convenience of the wealthy any more than it can bend to the ease of the poor.

It can be further argued that, given a somewhat unified and interdependent world market, which is yet to exist but which is in the making, growth in one end of the equation should be limited by the ability to balance growth at the other end. This is not a sympathetic notion to the current ethos of commercial and industrial activity, but it will be. If the greater good is truly part of any pan-governmental long-term plan, rules must exist not to exclude, but certainly to limit profit to boundaries of good business practices and human rights.

We are rapidly approaching a time when primary goods must reach fairer international value, and added value goods must be remunerated as a function of its intrinsic value. We must recoil to the system where pricing was merely a function of manufacturing and distribution costs as opposed to the model where market value has less and less to do with natural value.

If an encompassing global socioeconomic growth – the by-products of which will certainly be world peace – is ever to be attempted, it is through a fairness of pricing and profitability – incurring the barring of government subsidies, dumping, stocking of commodities for speculation, and other such artificial devices used to manipulate final market pricing – that it can be achieved. Most of all, the world can no-longer accept hegemonies that interfere militarily, and with intelligence facilities, to gain an economic edge over the others. In the age of globalisation, there must be limits to what can and cannot be brooked in the international arena.

The time for national egotism is past. We are economically and ecologically tied to one another for better or worse. Likewise, greed and insatiability must now give way to conscientious growth. We are not talking here of international charity. We are talking of keeping to the intrinsic value of things. We are talking of fair business practices and fair pricing of goods, without artificial and unfair manipulation. Let the maximisation of profits stop where the natural value of goods and services happens.

It is not a question of giving up wealth, as much as it is a question of analysing how much greed is required for the pursuit of happiness. We must not feel deprived of our richness when we adjust profitability to what is real and fair. We must realise instead that our happiness is interactive with the happiness of those surrounding us. Conflict can be deterred where common ground and shared wealth can be achieved.

Global society is at a crucial turning point in moral ethics. On one hand, there is the possibility of engaging the furtherance of an economic model that has been proven as a resilient and functional as it is heartless and destructive. We can take the model cracked by recent, and still ongoing, global economic crises and mend it so that the next crisis will be pushed further out. On the other hand, we are at the verge of discovering a new and yet untested model that will answer both to the ambitions of individuals and organisations, albeit within the boundaries of the realisation of the interdependency of national economies and the respect for human dignity.

One thing is certain in this scenario: On our joint decisions lie the future of humankind and the harmony of nations. Whether we will finally decide to build a more humane global society, or whether we will continue in our present path to its bitter end, is entirely up to our individual conscience, and consequently to our collective choice.

****

Chapter V

CURBING THE GOLDEN RULE

By now, I hope that the reader has realised that a focus on *"Self & Wealth"* is not fertile grounds for a harmonious and constructive society. Is this a novel thought? Perhaps not.

According to St. Thomas Aquinas – XIII century philosopher – it is weak will that allows a man to choose a standard allowing sensory pleasure to come ahead of one requiring moral constraint. Aquinas also attributed variances in moral guidelines to personal conscience to the weak-willed individual's incapacity of balancing their own needs with those of others. Where such weakness prevails, selfishness ensues and where there is selfishness, there is also ruthlessness, corruption and injustice.

Isn't that a little harsh? By Aquinas' principle, we today are all at fault because, in our society, and principally touching business affairs, we are taught to be anything but considerate of others' needs. We are instead taught to defend our own interests. Why is it so wrong to defend your interests in detriment of the interests of others? Wouldn't they do the same? This is a very personal question in ethics.

Yet, when we speak of ethics, what are we talking about? Aren't ethics just a social convention? Can't we just adjust ethics to make things work in practice? How permeable is our code of ethics to our convenience?

Ethics in general is seen academically as a branch of philosophy, with both timeless scholarly value and practical socioeconomic applications. Also known as *"Moral Philosophy"*, through ethics we attempt to define both the theoretical definition of concepts like *"goodness"* and *"propriety"* and the amount of truth in them, passing through the wider consequences and objectives of things like *"goodness"* and *"propriety"*, to culminate with a set of practical standards of *"what to do"*.

The theoretical side of ethics, represented by the field of Meta-Ethics, is mainly concerned with meaning and metaphysical repercussions of *"rightness"* and *"wrongness"*. It attempts to understand the greater truth behind moral values. The idea is to define them as factual and transcendental truth.

The transitional side of ethics is characterised in the field of Applied Ethics. Through Applied Ethics, an attempt exists to understand and conciliate the premises of deontology, utilitarianism and virtue ethics; or in other words, find the functional middle-ground between the following of rules of duty and morality, the understanding of causality and consequence and the pursuit of moral behaviour, through virtue, and for its own sake.

Finally, the practical side of ethics is found mainly in Normative Ethics, which in itself is a synthesis of Meta-Ethics and Applied Ethics. Therefore, Normative Ethics refers to the study and proposition of a functional code of conduct, based on ideas of correct and incorrect – or rather right and wrong – behaviour and their effects.

In the modern era and as early as in the XVII century, ethical theories were proposed via the duality of the consequentiality of actions – as proposed by utilitarian philosophers like Jeremy Bentham and John Stuart Mill – and mainly Kantian deontological ethics. The theories that flourished in the period known as the *Enlightenment* are also associated with more recent postulates such as the works of John Dewey. Dewey epitomised pragmatic ethics, of which the meaning deals principally in society's endowment to re-evaluate the expediency and truth of social morality, much in the same manner as scientists re-evaluate their theorems based on new evidence. Certainly, an intriguing notion.

Whether this is applicable in the human experience or not is still subject of debate. It would indeed be convenient to modern habits based on the maxim of consumerism that it was. Yet, historical, anthropological and sociological evidence sometimes suggest that Man has certain rigid inbuilt characteristics, which make Man's general behavioural tendencies less permeable to substantial change than Man's scientific knowledge. We are, after all, creatures endowed of more than a few persistent natural features[xvii].

Therefore, it is understandable that virtual, deontological and utilitarian approaches to morality are more frequently associated with practical studies than pragmatic ethics itself; though the latter certainly has its place in the sun. Be that as it may, whereas deontology judges the morality of any given behaviour, according to a set of laws, utilitarian ethics envisions the morality of actions based on the greater good as the ideal pragmatic objective. But taken together what does all this translate into?

I'm certain there are less simplistic understandings to which the reader can refer, but in my mind, the sum of modern ethical theories indicates that actions in general are morally justified if:

    A. They are performed within the customs, laws and statutes ruling the situation;
    B. They result in quantifiably greater contentment than disapproval;

> C. And their moral implications must be revised every now and again to suit new conditions and new findings, such as public opinion.

But is that really true? Is something *right* and *correct* solely because it obeys a set of arbitrary rules or because there are more people happy with the outcome than people dismayed by it? Is something that is truly *right* – and therefore also true – changeable according to the fluidity of historical context? I don't believe so.

Firstly, it would be necessary to question the validity of the rules. Who made them? On what principles are they based? How universal is the rule? Secondly, does it suffice to please the majority in order to obtain ethical justification? What if the majority is essentially misjudging the facts? What if they've been manipulated? Finally, if we uncover something that is truthful and correct, how mutable can it be? What profoundly different context could there be to quintessentially change the reality of our finding?

Imagine, if you will, a direct democracy where men and women had equal rights toward apprenticeship and practice of any profession, as well as equality of remuneration for services rendered. Then imagine that women represent sixty-percent of citizens living in that nation, being the majority over men.

By their rules, women could then vote to be entitled to collect twice as much payment as any man, for the same amount and quality of work. That would indeed be a situation where the rules of democracy were obeyed. Assuming their economy could withstand it, the resolution would even result in the greater good in the sense that more citizens would be benefited from the new directive than harmed by it. Yet, would it be fair? Would it be conducive to social harmony? Would it be morally right to afford women greater payment than men for no other motive than gender? On what grounds?

The subject could be argued, but it would certainly never find solid ground.

Here's another hypothetical example based on a frequent historical event: War. Assume that a bigger nation invades a smaller nation and conquers strategic territory, which traditionally belonged to the invaded nation. Imagine that the larger nation has clear laws permitting the initiation of hostilities and aggressive incursion into foreign soil, when resources found there are deemed essential for the survival of their natural population.

I now ask you: Morally, does it matter that the bigger nation's law allows for war? Does it matter that there are more people rejoiced with the event in the larger country than people dismayed by it in the smaller country? Will the taking of the territory become righteous if the new territory provides prosperity to the invaders? Will the fact that land was stolen from a people, via the use of brute force, become justifiable if we say the bigger nation will need the land for farming? Will it be right if we prove the invaded nation to be *"intrinsically evil"*?

Forcible relocation is another frequent dilemma. Can expelling small communities from their lands and their homes to suit the needs – and often just the interests – of a larger population be in any way morally, right? Again, the object of the dilemma is how worthy is the greater good and how moral are the laws behind such an action.

Under what circumstance will the need of the larger group be prevalent over the right of ownership of the smaller one? How large does a group of people have to be in order to make their forcible removal unjust or immoral? Should it follow that the concept be automatically translated to justifiable relocation of large industrial complexes and mining operations, in benefit of agrarian communities that feed the poor? Why not? What are the deontological and legal implications of this, especially where right to property is concerned?

These are questions that should haunt us each and all because we keep repeating such mistakes, over and over again, throughout history and even to-date. Note that we are not discussing a pragmatic need for survival nor any such notion. Nor are we discussing the justified use of brute force. We are indeed quite plainly speaking of invasion and expulsion of a people who, by our own laws, would be the rightful owners of a land. We are discussing something that governments and nations have perpetrated throughout history, under various allegations.

So, you see: Humankind perpetrates horrible immoralities and injustices for *"the sake of the greater good"* and we try to console ourselves by telling our aching consciences that it was the lesser of two or more evils. Yet we forget that there are no small evils. Such iniquitous actions invariably produce ripples in both history and in society, and these echoes have enduring harmful effects.

More to the point, if we look upon these controversial issues – whether individually or collectively – with any honesty, we'll find that we lie and we cheat and we mislead and let ourselves be deceived in the name of good things, but always with ulterior gains following hard behind our allegations to benefit ourselves or certain "someones". We set aside our own rules, our sense of right and wrong and our fear of the consequences whenever it suits us. Sadly, for all our advancement in law and technology, we have yet to tame ourselves, our conveniences and our voracity.

Nevertheless, instead of seeking to propose higher aims for Humanity as a whole, modern – and indeed contemporary – ethics seems to be content in justifying our errors. In fact, we are told by some thinkers[xviii] that we should revise our codes of conduct to better befit our natural failings. It seems that we are to accept the flaws in our nature because they are part of us. Should we really?

Let me put this in the context of contemporary aesthetics: Should we accept an ugly mole at the tip of our nose just because we were born with it? The honest reply will certainly be *"no."* Most contemporary women wouldn't brook the ugly mole if they could remove it. Most modern men wouldn't either. Nor would a plastic surgeon advise against the removal of the mole, would they? As well let us not deceive ourselves in saying that the hairy mole is beautiful. It is not. None of us deems it so. The same should apply to other facets of our nature, especially those that need taming.

As a species, we know full well what our failings are because they have not changed so much over the course of our history. They are repetitive and consistent everywhere because we are fairly regular in nature. They are ugly as sin.

Is the list very long? Yes certainly. If you turn them into words, the vocabulary list of our imperfections is even longer than the one for our perfections, which is good because this helps us ascertain our propensity to err.

Still, if I were to synthesise the full set of our common flaws in one phrase, I would say that they are *all the principal things preventing us from living with one another in perfect harmony.* This includes all forms and expressions of vanity, selfishness, greed, hostility, wickedness and contempt that would result in grievances.

So, you see, human failings abound and we indulge in them. Chief among them is greed though. At least I see it that way. The will to have more than you need and more than you deserve is behind many other evils perpetrated by mankind. It makes you pursue extravagance and accumulate what may be superfluous to you and indispensable to another. It generates vices and decadence. It makes you covet what isn't rightfully yours and act upon it. It pervades and corrupts as easily as it would destroy. It unfolds into an infinity of pain and suffering.

There is no virtue in being greedy. There is no effort, no merit and no betterment either, for it comes easily to us. In a sense, indulging greed is like breathing or defecating. It's just there: Inherent to our physiology. When you realise you're doing it, it's already happening. Yet nowadays, greed is often synonymous with ambition, and it is stimulated both by the ethics of profit and the mechanics of consumerism.

Nowadays it is amazing to think that personal greed was historically often seen as immoral. Whereas frugality and austerity are seen as virtues in many cultural and religious traditions, greed is invariably seen as something deplorable. In Christian societies of old it was even seen as a capital sin. Nonetheless, by revised modern standards, greed would be right if it were to be pursued within the law, and if it arithmetically resulted in greater quantity of satisfied people than displeased ones. Would that assessment clear your conscience? It doesn't clear mine.

To me, an act that obeys the letter of the law and simultaneously contents the majority is indeed commendable. Certainly, it is convenient, democratic even, but not necessarily right. Likewise, an act that is truly based on what is right for human nature cannot change over time, because human nature does not change as much as we would like to believe.

While human codes of ethics and human laws have indeed changed at times, over the course of our recorded history, I submit that our nature – the core of our being – is perennial. Our basic human yearnings and human physiology and the human mind have not changed very much in the course of recorded history, if they changed at all.

There is evidence enough to support this affirmation in literature and in history, if not in anthropology, archaeology and medical science. Certain themes and certain facts seem to occur everywhere where Man has set foot.

It makes sense. Since our bodies have not changed much, our functions are all still there, as they have been. The emotions and inherent faults of our ancestors are all still preserved in us.

It is folly to think that we today are paragons of humankind without historical precedent. It is unwise to believe ourselves the superiors of our predecessors in regards to self-awareness, for we have yet to tame our most basic instincts. Many of us don't even reflect about their actions. Many just do what comes naturally.

Unlike the preaching's of scepticism and relativism[xix] – and much of pragmatic ethics[xx] - I do believe that there is such a thing as absolute truth behind the moral values we should cherish. If not absolute in the cosmos, it will certainly be absolute for Humanity, which is really what concerns us at this point in time.

I therefore disagree with what philosophers in the vein of Joseph Margolis seem to advocate in the sense that, while he is more cautious than other defenders of relativism in admitting the reality of absolute truth, he still fails to acknowledge that there are indeed certain undeniable facts about the human condition that go beyond cultural and legal context.

There is a higher purpose than serving the will of the majority, via the laws of man, simply because we have failed to produce perpetual definitions of what the greater good really is, and because our laws are not always written for the purpose of the greater good. Too often in record have legislators produced laws to favour themselves and their supporters. Too often in the past have dictators promulgated laws to benefit a precious few acolytes and oligarchies. Are these even legitimate laws?

While I defend those laws, customs, and statutes are indispensable instruments of social order, I'm afraid that Humanity is frequently plagued with personal greed, and that society's public institutions are peppered by individuals of excessive ambition, and that these very human characteristics continue to sully our laws; repeatedly compromising their ability to promote justice and order.

I also submit that, for practical social intents, human nature is not as complex and varied as our desires and conveniences would have us believe; though it may subjectively appear so to us. It is not that our nature isn't intricate and diverse, but it is so on an intellectual level and not so much on a practical behavioural level. If you are familiar with the theories of Abraham Maslow, his followers and his critics, you may realise that most of us have simple needs, and we tend to act according to these first.

Maslow speaks of the *"hierarchy of needs"* with the physiological needs as the primary objective, the sense of security – or safety – follows and then the sense of belonging and esteem follow, as separate social aspects. The final priority is accomplishment – or self-actualisation – where Maslow includes achievements and moral issues. As I understand his views, Maslow refers to human nature as animal first, emotional second and only then intellectual.

Conversely, Dutch social psychologist and anthropologist Geert Hofstede has asserted that Maslow's hierarchy is subject to cultural differences, which in my view is plausible. Chilean economist and philosopher Manfred Max-Neef goes further into affirming fundamental human needs are non-hierarchical at all.

Be that as it may, whether hierarchy applies regularly, differentially or not at all, it is generally agreed that the average human being feels a need for subsistence, social acceptance, comfort and pleasure. If you are an average human being, and if you are honest with yourself, it is likely you will concur with that assessment.

Assuming this is basically true of human nature, I submit that, if left solely to our own resources, we make our decisions first and foremost based on these basic needs, whatever the priority we give to them. In fact, more often than not, we would devise a decision that suits our perception of our convenience even before we realise it. That decision made; we then proceed to formulate its justifications.

It is only at the point of justifying our decision – to ourselves and to society – that we are permeable to self-criticism and conscience. Sometimes this may even result in a reformulation of the decision. Yet, when acting on the spur of the moment, our impulse will normally have us act per our need for subsistence, comfort, social acceptance and pleasure. This is what comes naturally. The rest is self-imposed.

Self-imposed behaviour can be taught or it can be spontaneous. Whatever the case may be, with discipline and repetition, self-imposed behaviour can become second nature, and it may supplant natural instinct. We call this *"habit"*. This is not only common in social behaviour, but vital to communal living. In fact, it is of paramount importance to society that we do learn to impose barriers to some of our natural impulses. I don't think that any person of wisdom would disagree with that assessment.

Similar to the ability to self-impose control over bowel movements and other physiological functions, we humans have proven ability to control our basic urges and spontaneous drives. Saying that we don't can only sound like a delusion to excuse our choice for ravenous and libertine conduct.

We are indeed creatures partly driven by instinct and by hedonism and, as such, we are inherently self-serving. It is in our nature. However, if all of us were to submit to egotism and self-servitude, there would never be the possibility of communal living. In order for communities to arise, we must surrender some of our personal convenience and satisfaction that others may also enjoy theirs.

Alas, sharing territory and sharing resources is not something that comes easily to us. This is one classic and recurrent example of why ethics must aspire to greater purposes than deontology and utilitarianism. While the instinct toward self-preservation has aided in our survival and in prevailing against adverse conditions, whenever these conditions are no-longer exactly as threatening as they once were, the instinct must be put in check. We must teach ourselves to let go of the voracity and violence associated with self-preservation. This is mostly achieved through moral codes.

Bear with me: If you believe in Darwinism and the Theory of Evolution, then you must also believe that we are the product of a selection that imbued us with this imprinted impulse linked to self-preservation. Because of our evolution, Man is essentially a territorial creature. While we have a drive toward building communities, we also tend to protect ourselves and our pack and our territory against competition. It is in our temperament to protect our survival – and the survival of our herd – by ensuring we own territory and the resources in it. With survival at stake, we do this even in detriment of others. Nevertheless, can we say today that our survival depends principally on territoriality?

Territoriality and self-preservation are not evil things per se, but any person of good sense will admit that they can be conducive to wickedness at given extremes. This happens when another component enters into play, and this can be *"want"* as much as it can be *"greed"*. Many wars throughout our history have spurted out of this simple premise.

So, in essence, we have repeatedly succumbed to greed-imbued natural instincts, time and again, since the birth of history, and this has but reinforced these instincts and this behaviour. Nowadays we continue to do so as nations and as individuals, albeit in a disguised form. We dress greed with pseudo-ethics and logical justification so that we may perpetrate it, but it is still greed. We have relegated our higher intellect to the background, where it serves the purpose of justifying actions we chose based on our natural instincts.

As we've already seen, consumerist thought taps into this very human attribute, as well as the basic needs Maslow first identified. It is not a particularly complex concept to grasp and, in some societies, it becomes very evident. Crafty marketers meddle with these basic instincts, and entice via these basic needs, to provoke a response from the consumer. As consumers, most of us let it happen. We do it to feel good. We accept it because we get a fix from pleasing ourselves, and contemporary society imputes no relevant moral implications to self-satisfaction through consumption of legal goods.

We tell ourselves we are very complex beings, and we hide ourselves behind the claim that we do not fully understand our nature and the dynamics of our behaviour. We tell one another that because of our complexity and because of our differences, we must keep our options open. We say to ourselves we cannot fully determine a universal code of conduct for ourselves because we are very different from one another. Are we?

Whether this is in dispute or not, whether the complexity of human behaviour is an axiom impenetrable to us or not, there is a simple way of looking at our failings and a means to resolve them all with one swift stroke.

More than 2000 years ago it was said: "*Love your neighbour as thyself,*[xxi]" yet how much closer have we come to the Golden Rule than those who were Jesus of Nazareth's contemporaries? We are still striving with the concept, but it holds true. *"Do unto others as you would have them do unto you."*[xxii] This is a simple enough rule. It enables any person to subjectively evaluate a situation and derive a conscientious directive as to whether an action is just and right or not.

While it is arguably relativistic because it is based on self-awareness, perception and personal conscience, its flexibility will not transcend basic instinct of right and wrong; at least not in any sane individual.

Take the example of the unwillingness to die. Most of us have an innate instinct to protect our own life. Granted there exists a portion of the population that is capable of overriding this instinct, either via self-discipline or via a state of relative insanity, but the norm is that we all have the notion that *"dying"* is humanly undesirable. Under the Golden Rule, this realisation would mean that you would not endorse or impose any action that would jeopardise the life of any counterpart, just as you would not like your own put at risk. This translates into all forms of human suffering, as well as to the entire community that surrounds you.

If you stop to think of it, doesn't it make sense? Assuming you're a sane individual, whoever you may be, whatever your personal values and traditions, by honestly placing yourself in the position of the recipient of your actions, you can sense whether or not you are acting in good faith and whether or not your actions will be morally positive or at least justified.

Even if you wanted to impute a cultural paradox, it should still be possible for an informed individual to seek to understand the contextual controversy, and then analyse it subjectively – and in good faith – under the premise of the Golden Rule. Most of all in the *Age of Information*, anyone willing to try to understand how another culture thinks will find ample material available to that end.

In fact, this rule is so universally applicable to humankind that, at least according to Simon Blackburn[xxiii], the Golden Rule "*can be found in some form in almost every ethical tradition.*" In other words, it is the conclusion of almost every attempt of finding the truth behind our ability to live in harmony with one another.

Even if not present in all of our religious and philosophical traditions, the Golden Rule is clearly present in most of the more significant moral traditions of our history.

It is present in Confucianism: *"What you do not wish for yourself, do not do to others,*[xxiv]*"* Also, when Zi gong, a disciple of Confucius, posed: "*Is there any single word to guide a person throughout life?*" to which the master replied: "*How about reciprocity? Never impose to others what you would not choose for yourself.*[xxv]"

Mohism has it phrased by Mozi thus: "*If people regarded other people's families in the same way that they regard their own, who then would incite their own family to attack that of another? For one would do for others as one would do for oneself.*"

Taoism attributes the following to T'ai Shang Kan Ying P'ien: "*Regard your neighbour's gain as your own gain, and your neighbour's loss as your own loss.*"

The same concept is present in Hinduism, which is recognised as an amply relativistic religion: "*One should never do that to another which one regards as injurious to one's own self. This, in brief, is the rule of dharma. Other behaviour is due to selfish desires.*[xxvi]"

Similarly, Jainism prescribes: "*Just as pain is not agreeable to you, it is so with others. Knowing this principle of equality, treat other with respect and compassion.*[xxvii]"

Greek philosophy also embraced the concept. Plato had it as an ideal central to his philosophy: "*One should never do wrong in return, nor mistreat any man, no matter how one has been mistreated by him.[xxviii]"

It is present in Judaism, Christianity and in Islam with equal importance in each tradition. Judaism says: "*Do to no one what you yourself dislike.*[xxix]" Also: "*Recognize that your neighbour feels as you do, and keep in mind your own dislikes.*[xxx]" Again: "*That which is hateful to you, do not do to your fellow. That is the whole Torah; the rest is the explanation; go and learn.*[xxxi]"

Christianity has it again in the New Testament: "*Therefore all things whatsoever ye would that men should do to you, do ye even so to them: for this is the law and the prophets.*[xxxii]" And again: "*And as ye would that men should do to you, do ye also to them likewise.*[xxxiii]" The Great Commandment also refers to this Golden Rule: "*Love the Lord your God with all your heart and with all your soul. Love Him with all your strength and with all your mind. And love your neighbour as you love yourself.*[xxxiv]"

In Islam, we find it in both the hadith and the Qur'an. "*As you would have people do to you, do to them; and what you dislike to be done to you, don't do to them. Now let the stirrup go!*[xxxv]" Also: "*None of you believes until he wishes for his brother what he wishes for himself.*[xxxvi]" And also: "*Seek for humankind that of which you are desirous for yourself, that you may be a believer.*[xxxvii]" And again: "*The most righteous person is the one who consents for other people what he consents for himself, and who dislikes for them what he dislikes for himself.*"

Sikhism, another arguably relativistic doctrine, puts it thus: "*I am a stranger to no one, and no one is a stranger to me. Indeed, I am a friend to all.*[xxxviii]"

As you can see, the Golden Rule is universally agreeable in its elegant simplicity and in the truth of it. Yet we keep seeking for alternatives. Do we seek a better rule? One that is easier to follow or apply? I earnestly do not think so. I think instead that we are looking for a way around it.

What we really want is to satisfy our whims. We want to please our bodies and our spirits and our minds with anything and everything that they desire. Consumer society even tells us this is the right way. We want, as did our ancestors, to placate our instincts and to follow our nature to the letter, but we know there are negative consequences to this pursuit.

We have in our history and in our experience seen that where there are groups thriving in complacency and excess, others must endure privation and want. For hedonism to exist, those who can will rule, and those who can't must serve them with their own neglect.

This was, and still is, the reality of our society. An abnormally powerful ruling class prevails and enjoys a life of overindulgence – with their acolytes enjoying the ample scraps from their table – while multitudes languish in servitude.

Although this relationship once was a phenomenon privy to the borders of a nation, it is nowadays a global system. Whole nations tend toward intemperance and complacency, while entire peoples pay for it with a life of poverty and want. There is a prevailing imbalance – exacerbated in the ethics of profit and the democratisation of consumerism – that is morally corrupt, though we became comfortable with that corruption.

While individual conscience is soothed by a discourse of fallacious meritocracy and deceptive democracy, governments and oligarchies conspire to hide the perfidy behind the system. They hush the voices that would cry out the shame of a system that condones powers that are selfish and incongruent with human dignity. Through the ethics of profit, governments and oligarchies paint in the pastel colours of currency the raw red of human suffering and the black stain of environmental decay.

As for us, we let our governments pursue inequity – both foreign and domestic – in our name, as long as we can live out our lives in plenty. We let them because it is convenient to us. We let them because we are ourselves content to be what we are. We let them because we are bribed with civil rights, corporate benefits and facilities. We take our bribes and keep our tongues behind our teeth.

We already have an informed conscience that this course leads to the satisfaction of a few in detriment of the wellbeing of most. Collectively, we know for a fact that it culminates with human suffering and we want to personally dissociate our individual choices from responsibility over that overall result. We want to sate our yearnings alright, but we want to do it without guilt.

This is, in my understanding, the main stimulus for trying to curb the Golden Rule. It is also the principal motivator behind contemporary society's attacks on religious precepts, for religions have a way of contrasting with selfishness. Personal greed and personal complacency were and remain the driving forces behind the philosophical attempt to find a replacement for virtue ethics.

But what is virtue ethics?

* * * * * * *

Chapter VI

RETURN TO VIRTUE ETHICS

The term *virtue ethics* corresponds to the thought that desirable qualities and good character play a central role in moral action, and that they should be nurtured both individually and collectively. Under this notion, the agent of the action – you – are personally responsible and accountable for determining the laudable or reprehensible outcome of any action.

As commented in the previous chapter, virtue ethics is seen today as one of three predominating traditions in Moral Philosophy, the other two being *deontology* and *utilitarian consequentialism*. While deontology focuses on duty and normative rules as moral guidelines, consequentialism sees the outcome of actions as the parameter to moral decisions. In other words, deontology could be construed as the birthplace of most legal systems and utilitarianism feels akin to a Machiavellian line-of-thought, where the ends justify the means.

To make the distinction clearer, let's take a practical contemporary example: Piracy of intellectual property. If you accept piracy of intellectual property as the unlawful appropriation, reproduction and sale of material that another has generated, and over which another owns certain commercial rights, then you must accept that piracy is illegal, and therefore unethical. Yet, it is clear in measurable social behaviour that not everyone agrees with that assessment.

Some people seem to be very comfortable with the pirating of software, motion pictures, computer games, fashionable clothes etc. Why is that?

If we were to analyse this matter under the eyes of deontology – a philosophical view based on the following of rules – it would be clear that a contravention of the law reigning over intellectual property, and the subsequent illegal infringements of copyright, and of the laws that regulate commerce, would characterise intellectual piracy as an unethical and immoral act. Much of the argument made in commercials against piracy is based on this premise, isn't it?

Ironically, these deontological campaigns end up being targeted principally with those people who already purchased the original product, meaning that they probably already adhere to the notion that "piracy is stealing", as is so eloquently put on announcements included in almost every DVD sold for private entertainment. This fact may be part of why the campaigns that run with this concept are so obviously unsuccessful. Perhaps that's why new approaches such as "piracy is not a victimless crime" or even "they are having fun, while the other guy is wasting time in an illegal download" have been adopted.

Yet it could be said that these other ideas – which signify a departure from a purely deontological approach and a reproachment with utilitarian and pragmatic concepts – are also inherently flawed in the objective of suppressing the desire for pirated goods. This is because all of these ideas have the same inherent weakness: The moral restraints of the public in general have been corrupted. "By whom?" is the question that possibly hurts the most for some of those who are themselves the victims of piracy.

Be that as it may, in contrast with how deontology sees piracy, if we were to look at the issue under the pragmatic concepts of utilitarian ethics –philosophical theories aiming at promoting the greater good – an argument could be built to support piracy on the grounds that it is socially desirable. Shocking, isn't it? How can something illegal be desirable? Simple: The greater good demands it. Pragmatically speaking, if piracy were to be a source of social inclusion and a deterrent to violent crime, shouldn't it be tolerated? Under the light of utilitarianism, it might. Besides, piracy could be desirable not only on the basis of personal monetary gain, but also as a regulator to overvaluation of certain products and brands, principally those who bend ethics in social communication.

Marketing campaigns the world over have at times communicated, and continue to convey the message that people are only as good as what they materially boast, which in itself generates grievous undesirable social distortions. Commercials and other media often make the case that a particular item will make you into something better. They make the case that social acceptance and popularity revolve around ownership of certain trappings. What of those who can't buy them? How should they obtain such indispensable items? Piracy provides a way for these social strata that is less harmful than more violent crimes. In that sense, as a leveller of social injustice and preventer of violence, piracy could be found to be functionally desirable, couldn't it? Whether it should or not is another matter, one that relativism and utilitarianism may not solve.

In this sense, it is conceivable that there could be people who find themselves justified in consuming pirated products. They could appease their conscience by telling themselves that they are regular "Robin Hoods" of modern times, taking from the corrupting profiteering corporations to give to the poor – themselves mostly – and thus promoting a sort of social justice. That is certainly crooked reasoning according to deontological views, but it would be acceptable in utilitarianism, if a proper argument were to be built in favour of pirated goods standing against the distortions promoted by the "greedy corporations".

Finally, we could look at piracy with the eyes of virtue ethics – the philosophical tradition that seeks to promote ethical behaviour through personal worthiness – whereupon piracy would not be acceptable, even if it would be used specifically to supplant socioeconomic abuses by the wicked, even if promoting social justice without personal gain. Like in deontology, intellectual piracy would be deemed wrong by virtue ethics in any context, as it is a commandeering of the fruits of someone else's efforts, without permission; thus being morally reprehensive.

Though in this case the effect is the same as in deontology, virtue ethics disapproves of intellectual piracy mainly because it is a corruptive principle that would lead into other misbehaviours. That it is against the law is another matter. Hence, virtue ethics proposes a straightforward approach to address causes and consequences first, and only then a multifaceted one, with legal and practical implications. This distinguishes the doctrine from both deontology, which is mostly about following clear-cut rules, and utilitarianism, which is predominantly about finding intricate justifications for whatever you want to do.

Personally, I don't condone intellectual piracy. Yet I think the only way to resolve the issue with any justice is to correct its origins. I feel there needs to be a moralisation of social communications and the media in general, more common sense where royalties and profits are concerned, greater ethics in taxation and public spending, and certainly a change of paradigm away from consumerism, before the issue of product/brand piracy can be resolved.

Furthermore, I feel that these issues can only be unravelled if we take responsibility for them individually before we do so collectively. We must each individually have a conscience before we can have a law-abiding society. This is something virtue ethics approaches with a greater degree of propriety than either deontology or utilitarianism.

Let's be fair: A lot of the same companies that now complain about piracy have been working tirelessly to maximise profits, increase royalties and to teach people that their products and brands were incommensurately invaluable and that they'd be regarded as better people if they owned them, regardless of other factors. They've been at it for quite some time now. High pricing as a function of branding instead of practical utility is a common thing nowadays. Aren't they reaping what they sowed?

To begin to revert the issue, we should instead invest in telling people that they need to tend themselves more dearly and act more honourably. We should tell them that they need to cultivate a more moral frame of mind, and that your actions do indeed matter more than your possessions to define who you are. We should also lead by example and be ethical and moral companies and brands. Yet doing this entails sacrificing some of what consumerism stands for, along with profit margins and a lifetime of investment in creating a market of voracious consumers.

Critics of virtue ethics frequently point out that this philosophy focuses little on the action itself and too much on the agent of the action. It is also sometimes argued that virtue ethics is vulnerable to cultural understanding of good and evil, right and wrong, which may very well bring about a level of variation on the moral imputations of certain actions.

Yet what is the action without its agent? What is the inherent moral quality of the action without the intent and the will of the agent? What's more, there is congruence in central aspects of the human experience that remain universal in most, if not in every human cultural tradition.

I believe no civilization we've encountered on Earth would disagree that altruism, charity, courage, justice, generosity, gratefulness, honour, honesty, prudence, temperance, valour and other such traits are undesirable in a person. These are called *"virtues"* because they are qualities that make it easier for people with our nature to live together. They are traits of excellence at being human, at the best interpretation of what being human can be.

Equally, arrogance, avarice, brutality, disloyalty, envy, grudge, hate, hypocrisy, irresponsibility, intolerance, indiscretion, indolence, presumption, profligacy, rudeness, selfishness, short-sightedness, tactlessness, ungratefulness, vanity, vengefulness and many more such notions seem to be unanimously unwelcome, but by a few sub-cultures and some recent developments. This is so because they are attributes that make it more difficult for the maintenance of harmony among people.

A person that indulges in such vices regularly would indeed run the risk of being classified as arrogant, avaricious, brutal, disloyal, envious, grudging, hateful, hypocritical, irresponsible, intolerant, indiscrete, lazy, presumptuous, reckless, rude, selfish, short-sighted, insensitive, ungrateful, vane, vindictive etc. as would their actions.

It has been argued as well that these words that we use to define virtues and vices find different meaning throughout different social strata and before historical context. Yet this is a doubtful argument, in that the idiomatic uses and misuses of terms will not defeat the meaning intended, when one speaks philosophically of the moral notion itself. It is not because the word *"honour"* may have diverse legal and cultural interpretations, that the meaning of honour as a *"virtue of fortitude of character and magnanimity"* will cease to exist or cease to be pertinent, when one speaks of it in the context of morality.

Semantics notwithstanding, it is clear that there are common grounds regarding conduct conducive to favourable responses and outcomes and conduct contributing to disaster and disfavour. As to the truth behind the conduct, there is still much philosophical debate in that regard. Some argue that true virtue only happens out of authentic inclination, while others hold that learned virtue is as truthful as authentic virtue, where I tend to agree, at least insofar as when the virtuous attribute becomes second nature.

Naturally, it is agreeable to foster positive conduct from spontaneous good will, for it will be genuine and true, and as something genuine and true, it will be likelier to endure than an artificial positive behaviour. Yet I dare venture that when that authentic good conduct is not realistic, it is socially preferable to obtain positive conduct from customs and uses, then it would be to suffer negative behaviour.

I submit that, while deontology and consequentialism certainly offer complementary and useful philosophical views to virtue ethics, virtue ethics has traditionally been the prevailing Moral Philosophy in western culture for a reason. For instance, whereas Plato and Aristotle are often pointed as the founding fathers of the idea, virtue ethics' roots in Chinese philosophy are even more ancient than those found in Classical Antiquity. That it has expressions in many cultures and traditions speaks for itself, as to how universal the concept that virtues should exceed vices really is for human experience.

Alas, starting in XVII century Europe, during the period we call the *Age of Reason*, virtue ethics was branded derogatorily as a dogmatic and theocentric view, and was cast aside in benefit of the more anthropocentric philosophical ideals, gathered under the term's deontology and utilitarianism. It would not be until the 1950's that virtue ethics would find a resurgence in Anglo-American philosophy; notably in Anscombe's celebrated 1958 article *"Modern Moral Philosophy"*.

At the time of Elizabeth Anscombe's[xxxix] treatise, there was an increasing dissatisfaction with the prevailing forms of utilitarianism and deontology, as they lacked a more meaningful understanding of true happiness. As well, pure deontology and fundamental utilitarian views seemed inadequate to answer issues that virtue ethics had long addressed. Topics such as the role of emotions and character, non-objective relationships, motives, moral wisdom and the issue of conscience were largely ignored in modern and post-modern philosophical conventions. Even so, virtue ethics' resurgence did not result in the extinction of the other currents, rather it influenced them to incorporate virtue theory in their own make.

Today, virtue ethics concentrates on recognising and cultivating desirable qualities, as a means of propitiating morally correct outcomes. The idea is to build a moral individual, with moral habits, thereby favouring moral conduct.

This is not as inflexible an idea as the adhering to a rigid set of rules, and it is not as malleable a concept as adjusting morality to the prevailing idea of what the conveniences of the moment entail. Instead, it is flexible enough to admit some adaptation to circumstance – mainly based on individual conscience and intent – and it is resilient enough to dismiss moral corruption because of the limits imposed by the virtues themselves.

For example, if we agree that loyalty is a desirable trait, we may agree that a loyal individual may sustain multiple allegiances, or different level commitments, befitting different scenarios, and remain true to the concepts of fidelity, faithfulness and trustworthiness, but we can never agree that a loyal person may conscientiously perform an act of outright betrayal and remain morally justified. Even if the disloyalty had been instrumental for the good of the majority, even if duplicity had been committed against a party not formally aligned with the agent, it would be morally reprehensible in itself, because whatever the treachery, it is never loyalty. Faced with a conflict between allegiances, if there are no alternatives to betrayal of at least one commitment, and mitigating circumstances notwithstanding, the agent would have wronged both the concept of loyalty and of prudence, for that agent would have entered two conflicting covenants.

Another example may be found in honour when it is defined as a virtue of nobility of soul. While honourable behaviour may implicate an unyielding stance to protect an innocent from injustice, it may also involve the yielding of pride in defence of the greater good. As such, honour is not a stagnant moral standpoint. Indeed, honour is quite permeable to circumstance, intent and conscience. Yet, an honourable person may under no condition surrender conscience, character or will for personal gain, for by doing so they'd be acting dishonourably and therefore also deplorably.

Honesty is also a widely recognised virtue even today. Honest individuals are normally seen as those who consistently keep their covenants, and who are consistently truthful. Yet it must be said that a truly honest person will heed the spirit of the law first and then the letter of the law, without dismissing the latter idly. Neither one nor the other should be discarded to suit the moment, but the first must supplant the second.

So, by this premise, an honest person can hold his tongue rather than commit an act of indiscretion that could be potentially harmful to someone, and still remain honest. The honest salesman can decide to price his products in a manner consistent with their nature and their purpose, and remain honest even if the price will afford him much profit. Yet, an honest person cannot be contented in divulging an inaccuracy or witnessing one and remain silent, in detriment of someone's wellbeing, and an honest salesman cannot price his products unfairly to their properties and still be morally justified, for in doing so he would become both harmful and dishonest in the view of his interlocutors.

In the final analysis, this concept propitiates emotional and motivational flexibility up to a point, and then quintessential consistency prevents corruption of the spirit of virtue in any action. This, to me, is fitting with what society requires. There needs to exist some level of malleability to allow for emotional and purposeful differences and accommodations, but this cannot be limitless; for any boundless flexibility is conducive to relativistic vice and social turmoil.

Furthermore, there must be accountability. There must be consistency between what is professed, what is intended and what is in fact delivered. Only then can there be moral truth to any action. Without moral truth standing behind each individual's choices, there can be no social harmony.

For society to thrive there must be a sense of collective collaboration toward that common goal. Cooperation and personal responsibility for the common good must be imbued in the vast majority of the social community.

Putting it in plain words: Egotism is contrary to harmony. People must begin to understand that what is good for everyone is consequentially good for them, but what is good for them is not necessarily good for everyone. This very concept precludes the possibility of limitless moral flexibility. This truth is even more so in face of adversity.

While a degree of elasticity is desirable for the inclusion of the diversity of human character, if moral codes exist – amongst other things – to enable the weaving of the fabric of society, then it is of immeasurable importance that they be reliable and constant, so as to offer guidance to social behaviour. Whatever the applied field, a relative – and therefore fluctuating – code of ethics will inevitably result in confusion and conflict; for if each person procures only their own convenience, there can be no agreement on a general arrangement.

What this translates into is the fact that one person's – or one group's – convenience is often actually inconvenient to another, to the level where conflict arises. So, if we allow moral parameters to be congruent with conveniences, clashes will become inevitable. Whether this is obvious, transgressions of this principal social relationship have been, and remain, common even in the diplomatic, political and legal spheres.

Through the eyes of virtue ethics, the ends will not justify the means if the means defeat the ends in the collateral harm that they produce. As people in general are already naturally bent on justifying individual and collective decisions according to their conveniences, we must at one point or another coerce these conveniences; else we incur the risk of establishing a state of social chaos. If anything is justifiable given a purpose – whatever it may be – then the risk and incidence of collateral damage all but increases. For society to endure in peace, there can be no moral recompense to acting in disharmony with the Golden Rule.

Whereas virtue ethics recognises the duality of human nature, it does propose this limit. It accepts that we are partly flesh and blood, with all that it entails in terms of passions, urges and needs, and it admits that we are also spiritual and intellectual beings. It acknowledges that the animal within exists, and it recognises that we normally have domain over it.

This is a premise of paramount importance, for it is well suited to the reality that each of us faces. We are creatures of both tangible and ethereal nature, and the former is no less worthy than the latter, but it cannot prevail. We should acknowledge that we need both of our natural forces, in order to experience our complete nature. We need both to overcome the perils of our existence and exert control over our intemperance. We draw strength from both our physical and our intellectual/metaphysical being. We grow out of the contention that exists between them. Yet, if we are to exist as a society, mind and spirit cannot submit to flesh; especially not in all moral things. If it does, the result is almost always collectively regrettable.

This is the offer a contemporary proposition of virtue ethics should contemplate. Society desperately needs individuals to have a moral anchor to prevent them from drifting in the contradictory currents of relativism. If there is to be social harmony, in addition to legality, there must be a voluntary sense of morality – a sense of both rectitude and accountability – to guide individuals in their choices. This has to be cherished above personal gain, and certainly above material wealth.

* * * * * * *

Chapter VII

THE QUESTION OF CONSCIENCE

What is conscience, and why should we act by it? For one thing, conscience is the voice of your own frame of reference. Sin against your conscience and you will be going against your personal views and feelings, the consequence of which is you'll be nagging yourself about it, at the back of your mind, and this is not a healthy prospect.

If you think you can escape this unkind judgement, you're mistaken. You can change your mind and bend your values on the surface, but deep within you are whole and true to your roots. This ingrained characteristic of our subconscious is more resilient than most of us acknowledges. The result of establishing a contention between your ego and your superego is often disastrous.

Conscience is a person's greatest judge, for it has insight into what you know about yourself and into every situation you transgress. Your conscience knows the true reasons for your transgressions just as you do, even if you chose to lie to yourself, even if you choose to ignore your own codes. You can deceive it just as you can betray yourself, but in truth it will be of no use. Your conscience knows all about what makes you tick. Act against it, and it will nag you into nightmares and great personal discomfort. Resist it, and it may change you into a bitter and sordid person. It doesn't matter what you tell others. It doesn't really matter what you tell yourself; at least at first. If you acted in contradiction with your conscience, you'll know about it and that is a ticket into psychological torment.

Formally, conscience is variously defined as a *"talent"*, a *"faculty"*, an *"insight"*, an *"intuition"* or some form of *"intellectual ruling"* that distinguishes right from wrong in your mind. While morality derives from established norms or implicit values, scruples are characterised rather by a *"gut feeling"* or a *"voice within"*, which informally defines conscience for many people. It is shaped by things beyond our active control, yet it is still subjective.

If you are a religious or otherwise spiritual person, then you must also believe in the metaphysical properties of conscience as a means of divine inspiration toward harmony. If this is the case, then sinning against your conscience is an even graver ordeal, for it entails that you either didn't trust it or you decided it was in your best interest to confront it. In either case, this would constitute a bad omen.

A religious analysis of the theme usually connects this human facility both to divine influence – or a benevolent cosmos, if you prefer – and to innate human morality; sometimes alluding to some form of natural law. In religion, violating conscience often entails a sin, because of the relationship between conscience and morality and morality and harmony among people. Diversity in doctrinal and ritual traditions notwithstanding, religions seem to agree that the voice of our conscience has both a natural and a metaphysical aspect, as well as an important moral function.

Surprisingly, contemporary scientific views pertaining to the mechanics of conscience certainly agree with religious views, insofar as acknowledging the probability of a natural feature to the origin and operation of conscience, as well as its social role. However, though secular views tend to link conscience to genetics – thereby establishing the natural aspect of the sense of right and wrong – some currents prefer to leave it at that, while others add environmental influence to account for the content of an individual's scruples instead of a divine feature.

Putting it into Information Technology terms, scientists largely believe genetics would supply the hardware of conscience, while culture and education would supply its software. This is sound theory, even if it remains unproven.

Charles Darwin, XIX century naturalist, suggested that "*any animal whatever, endowed with well-marked social instincts, the parental and filial affections being here included, would inevitably acquire a moral sense or conscience, as soon as its intellectual powers had become as well, or as nearly as well developed, as in man.*"[xl] Whether Nature would replicate the synthesis of conscience in other species just as it purportedly has done in Man is merely food for thought, Darwin's point does propose a furthering of a *"natural tendency"* toward the origin of conscience. He also unequivocally links our sense of right and wrong to our intellect, which may or may not be the case.

The XX century physicist Albert Einstein seems to have alluded to an *"inner voice"* as a source of knowledge both objective and moral. I refer to him here more as a self-professed supporter of humanist rationalism than scientist, as his expertise was not in genetics or the study of human behaviour. Nevertheless, notable scientist that he was, he is reported as having said: "*Quantum mechanics is very impressive. But an inner voice tells me that it is not the real thing. The theory produces a good deal but hardly brings one closer to the secrets of the Old One. I am at all events convinced that He does not play dice.*"[xli]

Einstein also regarded as *"enlightened"* a religious person whose conscience appoints that he "*has, to the best of his ability, liberated himself from the fetters of his selfish desires and is preoccupied with thoughts, feelings and aspirations to which he clings because of their super-personal value.*"[xlii] What this indicates is first that he acknowledges conscience as a faculty beyond the intellect. Secondly, he addresses the fact that there is a relationship between conscience, true freedom and altruism, to which he attributes an ostensibly higher status.

Psychology – on the other hand – often identifies conscience as the set of mental factors leading either to a sense of reward for acting with rectitude and in conformity with the norm, or to a sense of guilt for actions a person executes that transgress their moral values. In Psychology, conscience is sometimes alluded to social context, and sometimes to genetics and Darwinian Evolution Theory[xliii].

Some notable psychologists seem to identify conscience in much the same manner, as I've identified the uses of a moral code in relation to society in general. Sigmund Freud, for instance, viewed conscience as an attribute serving the purpose of inhibiting external expression of aggression and originating as a function of organised civilisation. Freud claimed that both the cultural and individual superego conspired to constitute ideal moral demands from behavioural decisions. Also according to Freud, the consequence of not obeying our conscience is remorse, which can lead to neurosis and an assortment of other negative behaviours.

Correspondingly, Philosophy sees conscience more times than not as a heritage of social frameworks, values and aspirations. However, how influential conscience can be in determining one's actions and how much it bases itself in ethics and in rational thoughts has been, and is still seen, as something highly debatable amongst philosophers.

In the XIII century, the philosopher St. Thomas Aquinas imagined conscience as the judicious application of moral awareness to instances of our lives. Rather than exclusively divine inspiration, he attributed personal participation in one's own conscience. He saw conscience as an act of reason originating in a natural human instinct for goodness and progressing, as an acquired habit, in day-to-day practical decisions. The influence of conscience would happen more and more – or less and less – as the individual voluntarily indulged the instinct for good or denied it.

Aquinas reasoned that acting in contradiction with one's own conscience is an intrinsically evil act, though acting in error is only culpable insofar as it results from deliberate ignorance. He deemed that there were things of which the individual had an obligation to make himself aware, which indicates our capacity to manipulate our own conscience instead of confronting it. He is even reported as deeming conscience an imperfect process of judgment because knowledge of the natural law was often-times obscured by selfishness, which in turn was promoted in customs serving social hedonism. In that sense, St. Thomas Aquinas further posed that conscience should be taught to seek real goodness – goodness derived from God, which is a kind of goodness that supports human development – rather than the obvious "*goods*" of sensory pleasures.

A more contemporary philosopher, Peter Singer[xliv], plays with semantics a little. He holds that describing deeds as "*conscientious*" normally indicates simply that we either mean to deny an action was motivated by egotism, or that it was performed on a whim, where he is often correct. In his utilitarian views, conscience also seems to appear in the subconscious understanding of most as an inhibitor to selfish desires, including greed, ambition and wickedness.

After all the debate, at the end of the day, it seems none can yet tell whether conscience is purely formed from an individual's upbringing and education, or whether it is simply inherited somehow via our DNA, or both taken together with the third element of divine influence also being a factor. To my knowledge, there are points of view supporting all of these theories, and debatable evidence indicating that one may be right over the other and vice-versa. The theme has been on the table for ages, and it is still under discussion both philosophically and scientifically.

However, as you can see from the opinions presented here, there is a pattern emerging among the differential analysis of all these diverse human disciplines. There are congruencies and converging thoughts regarding conscience. Whether practical, philosophical, scientific, theological or spiritual, in all these views there are common factors such as:

A. Conscience is a strong personal voice;

B. Conscience is part of a broader human context;

C. Conscience is socially invaluable;

D. Conscience helps us defeat selfishness;

E. Conscience is violable;

F. Conscience is vulnerable to education;

G. Conscience is fallible if not tended.

While the truth about conscience is still undiscovered, I feel free to believe it is an amalgam of both an inherited trait and an apprehended code, which in conjunction would – by no means – preclude divine inspiration, as this can come either metaphysically or through natural expression of the will of the Creator. Certainly, whatever the origin and mechanics of it, conscience is a powerful ingrained device capable of subjective insight, abstraction and apparent objective counsel. That it exists is the important point. That it is individual and non-transferrable is also relevant.

One may well claim that *"he did as others did,"* or that *"he followed orders,"* or even that *"he acted in accordance to the law,"* but in the end, these are mere devices to satisfy public and private ethics. The Human Race seems to have been aware of this for centuries; perhaps millennia.

An excerpt from William Shakespeare's HENRY V; Act 4, Sc.1, provides a little light on the subject, as approached by XVI century morality. Here, the king is in disguise amongst his troops upon the eve of battle against a more powerful antagonist. He partakes in a philosophical/theological debate with his soldiers, one of which has claimed that the king, having caused the battle to be, should inherit all the sins of the men under him. To this, the king says:

> *"So, if a son that is by his father sent about merchandise do sinfully miscarry upon the sea, the imputation of his wickedness by your rule, should be imposed upon his father that sent him: or if a servant, under his master's command transporting a sum of money, be assailed by robbers and die in many irreconciled iniquities, you may call the business of the master the author of the servant's damnation: but this is not so: the king is not bound to answer the particular endings of his soldiers, the father of his son, nor the master of his servant; for they purpose not their death, when they purpose their services. Besides, there is no king, be his cause never so spotless, if it come to the arbitrement of swords, can try it out with all unspotted soldiers: some peradventure have on them the guilt of premeditated and contrived murder; some, of beguiling virgins with the broken seals of perjury; some, making the wars their bulwark, that have before gored the gentle bosom of peace with pillage and robbery. Now, if these men have defeated the law and outrun native punishment, though they can outstrip men, they have no wings to fly from God: war is his beadle, war is vengeance; so that here men are punished for before-breach of the king's laws in now the king's quarrel: where they feared the death, they have borne life away; and where they would be safe, they perish: then if they die unprovided, no more is the king guilty of their damnation than he was before guilty of those impieties for the which they are now visited. Every subject's duty is the king's; but every subject's soul is his own. (...)."*

Shakespeare's opinion – one with which I tend to agree – indicates that a person cannot escape responsibility over their acts, even when they are commanded to pursue them. In summary, the notion is that whether you blame your actions on social context, on hierarchy or on the prevailing rules of the times, ultimately the decision was yours. You acted according to what you deemed desirable or acceptable or even necessary. That it was right and justified may or may not be relevant; it may or may not be the case. You made a call and pursued it. Now, you must deal with it. You must live with your decision and either relish in it or make amends. This includes reaping benefits or – more significantly – facing consequences, whereupon most people falter. Facing the consequences of your decisions – in particular of poor decisions – is what makes conscience and accountability reciprocally important.

Alas, the famous critic of current economic arguments, John Ralston Saul[xlv], articulates that, in developed nations, significant portions of contemporary society are beginning to surrender their sense of right and wrong to technical experts selected by "official" consensus.[xlvi]

In other words, the general gender seems to prefer that the choices be made for them. For most, social responsibility is reserved to the sporadic act of voting, which furthers the idea of delegating conscience and responsibility to others. According to Ralston Saul, by abiding to the *"conscience"* of specialists and authorities, free persons are voluntarily limiting their freedom of choice to a tiny spectrum of consumer actions, which in turn are ruled by the prevailing ideology convenient to the free market.

This is a fearsome prospect. It indicates that people are willing to be cattle. It indicates that they feel it is convenient to set aside their scruples, and with them any sense of guilt for what they themselves may deem as wrongdoing. People seem eager to do as they are told, shedding the blame for the outcome. The attempt may seem ludicrous in face of the unavoidability of dealing with one's own conscience, but it casts a palpable shadow over the future of society in general. Will we be a society ruled by a handful of opinions without even questioning them? This is a subject that has me worried.

Just as well, it cannot be ignored that there exist several scientific and philosophical currents nowadays that attempt to prove that neither *"conscience"* nor *"free will"* actually exist. The argument is very competently constructed around facets of human physiology and of Evolution Theory. However, it sometimes feels as if these theories are embraced as an apologetic approach to hedonism and rampant consumerism. At the very least, as an attempt to exempt the individual of responsibility for their acts, these theories are infertile towards the end of improving social relationships.

Building their case largely on experiments in neurolinguistics and other neuro-sciences, gentlemen in the vein of Sam Harris[xlvii] seem to try to invalidate the concept of *"free will"* altogether, which in turn is commonly interpreted as the absence of *"culpability"* and consequently the absence of *"moral"* implications to one's acts. However, this view falls short of arguing away *"choice"* as an inherent individual ability of any competent human being, regardless of where in the decision-making process it may happen.

Whether experiments carried out with the use of an fMRI appear to prove that, in some level or another, our choices are influenced by subconscious devices, and whether it can indeed be argued that *"ideal free will"* is impractical, it appears to me that the results of the experiments themselves, as well as the rationale that the array of our choices is limited, at the same time, by the world around us, by our genetic and subconscious inclinations, by the choices of others and the choices made before our time, the fact remains that, when presented with a problem, we command a fair level of autonomy to decide between the options available to us, in the manner that is available to us. We are therefore accountable at least for that level of choice, which is what matters to our practical human condition.

Regrettably, whereas many in the general gender self-servingly rush to hold-on to this idea that we are not imbued of free will, most appear to do so out of the desire to let go also of moral responsibility over their choices, as if by doing so they'd undo the practical consequences that may occur. It must indeed be said that the logic that without free will we are also without blame over what we pursue is sound. However, it is also false and very dangerous.

If we are honest with ourselves, at some level we intellectually and intuitively acknowledge that the assertion about the inexistence of practical free will is false, for we are quite aware that we each have at least some part in our decisions, and as such we are each morally accountable for no less than that part. It is dangerous in the sense that disregarding culpability will likely lead to selfish pragmatism and the decay of society into anarchy, for without moral accountability nothing exists to stop us from pursuing our self-servitude, except perhaps brute force.

At the end of the day, in the context of societal human relationships, it is quite clear that we have, to whatever degree, both the freedom to choose between alternatives accessible to us, and the obligation to accept responsibility over our choices. More to the point: For society to be viable and productive, we need the individual to be accountable for their acts and their choices. Yet, as a society and as a global economy, we seem to want to deny this. We even produce scientific research to prove that we are not liable for our decisions, and that history and our DNA are to blame in our stead. That is a worrisome realisation.

Just as Thomas Aquinas had cautioned in the XIII century, people nowadays are trying to deceive their conscience by remaining purposefully ignorant of the causes and consequences of their acts. They appear to do so in order to try to get away with going against their own sense of right and wrong by avoiding even having scruples. Indeed, it seems people nowadays are trying to do away with conscience altogether by denying its existence and by delegating it to others.

Who are these others? It matters not. Whoever they may be, their credentials notwithstanding, they are men and women as permeable to the temptations of our times as the next person. Experts as they may be in their respective fields, they are themselves influenced by contemporary opinions and the fluid ideology of a market, which is ruled by the stigma of continuously growing profits. At the end of the day, they are fallible. Still, the public seems content in abiding by their criterion just to shed the onus when things go awry.

We are talking here of a society that more and more desires to become a hive, with a hive's mental network. Society seems comfortable to delegate all its main decisions to a leadership, let these decisions filter down to the masses via intermediary soldiers, and see them implemented mindlessly by drones, who in turn are fed sweet honey to remain docile. The entire context reminds me of H. G. Wells' *"Time Machine"*. Is the average citizen like the Eloi waiting passively for Morlocks to come?

Yet the truth remains that the integrity of a person is a reflection of their conscience. Consequently, the integrity of a society of persons is a product of the predominating ethos, which is ultimately itself a product of the individual consciences of the people integrating it. Take away individual conscience, and you take away personal integrity. Take away personal integrity, and you sacrifice human distinction.

Without integrity, society succumbs to pragmatism and disintegrates.

People must realise they cannot have both blamelessness and choice. It is impossible to have both unaccountability and personal dignity. Surrendering your own conscience means losing your distinctive personality; your identity. Delegating your moral decisions to the prevailing idiosyncrasies of the times means submitting to the conveniences of the ruling ideology. It means enslaving yourself to the conveniences of rulers and tycoons, which often enough occur in detriment of the majority and even your own. We cannot have both a free humanist society and a mindless one. We cannot have both the liberty to be continuously self-indulgent and the semblance of social order. We must choose, and this choice must be a conscientious one.

If humankind is to endure, the individual cannot surrender their conscience to whomsoever they would. We must take responsibility for our lives and our decisions. We must act according to our judgement and face the consequences honourably, for only then we will be privy to the positive ripples of our acts. This is the only way to right the wrongs that we see proliferating all over the world.

* * * * * * *

Chapter VIII

THE UNIVERSAL UTOPIA

Only a society of conscience and virtue can promote world peace, a lasting stable economy and enduring multicultural harmony.

Why? Simply because only by creating virtuous and conscientious people – people capable of solidifying a moral system of relationships, conducive to interpersonal and inter-organisational trust, and capable of both independent self-respect and super-personal aspirations – will we be encouraging local development simultaneous to transcontinental confidence, mutual respect and positive diplomatic constructivism.

An individual who is capable of understanding the value of personal integrity, interpersonal justice and intercultural respect, out of experience, is the perfect agent to pursue institutional improvement, growth and the building of bridges and compromises. A society where there is a prevalence of such individuals will be one that functions with less obstructions, and will be able to grow solidly to seek continual improvement.

A society of conscience – one made from prudent, deliberate and liable citizens – is a responsible one. It seeks long-term solutions to its problems, not successive palliative short-term remedies. It procures the perennial welfare of its citizens, not demagogic and proselytised benefits. It promotes dependable economies based on realistic growth rates and tangible wealth, linked to social improvement, because it recognises that only such an environment will be sustainable across decades.

What's more, social responsibility begins with personal responsibility. When individuals are held accountable for their acts, and when the community embraces the laudable and rewards the honourable, the implication is that people will nurture a desire towards honour, valour and general worthiness. The ideal society must support and reward individual virtuous behaviour, so that collective conduct also becomes righteous. This is the premise that faces us on the threshold of trans-humanism. The ideal society is not a society made of masses, but of personal individuals. It is a society not devoid of individual identity, but replete with human dignity. Improve the person, and you shall distinguish a people.

Take away profits as the only institutional goal, and take away material wealth as the only mechanism of personal success, and replace them with society itself as the goal. Build an ideal of community and brotherhood and mutual respect that can justify existence instead of personal gain. Align it to an ideal of personal nobility, self-awareness and self-respect, as something above monetary gain, and you will create a citizen.

Here do we find our recipe. Recreate personal accountability and reinstitute individual honour, and you shall have spotless and efficient organisations. Promote professional pride, and true sustainable growth ensues based on quality and performance; not on pricing battles. Operate on truth, and you shall have trust. Fulfil promises, and you will have the beginnings of true credit, based on personal reliance, rather than collateral guarantees. Enhance the individual that the nation may flourish. Build a trustworthy and dependable human being, and you will have the building blocks of a society and an economy that can both be perpetually functional.

Above all, the Golden Rule should be the maxim of this ideal society, and it should be composed of these two factors:

A) Don't visit onto others what you would not like visited upon yourself;

B) Do onto others what you would like done for yourself.

It should follow that every citizen would, from a very early age, be taught to abide by this proactive binary principle of respect and civility. There can be no negative result that could possibly overcome the good that would flow from it to the ideal society, in every aspect of human co-existence.

Along with this essential principle, certain personal virtues should be encouraged so as to build an individual both serviceable and dignified that would contribute positively to form a harmonious community and a functional progressive society. Among the personal virtues that should be instituted and cherished in order to create the ideal society, we should contemplate:

I. Austerity & Frugality - instituted as a divorce from excess and the valorisation of simplicity – without incurring misery – will undeniably be instrumental in restraining egotism and in promoting long-term socioeconomic and environmental sustainability, by limiting generalised extravagance and reducing waste;

II. Duty - instituted in the civil sense to balance civil rights with civil obligations and service to the community, in conjunction with altruism, to facilitate harmony within society;

III. Honesty & Justice - instituted as general fairness in interpersonal and inter-organisational dealings will promote more objective and unobstructed personal and

professional relationships, enabling a maximisation of efficiency and a more harmonious environment;
IV. Honour & Dignity - would be important in establishing a personal identity away from material possession and closer to personal bearing and accomplishment;
V. Industry - instituted as tenacity, professional pride and hard work, and opposite profiteering and usury, to provide people with a sense of purpose, and to enable a resilient and sustainable economy based on productive relationships, and devoid of artificial finances, illusory wealth and creative book-keeping devices;
VI. Prudence & Common Sense - instituted as temperance of judgement with conscience, clemency and a sense of practicality to instil social understanding, tolerance and flexibility;
VII. Philanthropy & Altruism - instituted as a sense of community and collaboration toward the common good, including civil duty, selflessness and voluntary service to promote social justice and opportunity, and to combat selfishness and socioeconomic recklessness;
VIII. Loyalty - to be instituted as the basis of community and family and to enable honesty and duty;
IX. Valour - as the institution of the courage to do what is proper and right and to follow one's own conscience, despite outside pressure.

In the ideal society, these virtues would be generally deemed praiseworthy and would find incentives, both practical and social, in order that the public in general would incorporate and cherish them; growing fond of them both for their direct and indirect benefits.

The community in general would be invited to recognise personal achievement and individual virtue, in the form of admiration and esteem. Instead of offering these advantages as a function of wealth and luxury, the ideal society should afford them as a function of merit proven through virtuous behaviour and altruism.

Public-sector incentives could also come in the form of practical benefits, such as temporary privileges and tax reductions, offered to exemplary citizens and institutions, based on a yearly prize quota for philanthropy and outstanding achievement.

Private-sector incentives would come mainly through recognition and praise, but also as perks and bonuses offered voluntarily to worthy members of the community, for the service they render to society. These could be either tangible or intangible benefits that can make individuals feel recognised in their efforts.

Such ample incentives notwithstanding, the virtues would also find their way into the hearts of the populace via common sense. This, of course, must start with education. The ideal society must therefore be constructed with teachers, tutors and mentors as the most prestigious positions in all of the social hierarchy; above that of politicians, entertainers and such others. As such, teachers should be handsomely rewarded.

Here I make the distinction between remuneration and reward without saying that teachers must go on earning less than football players, movie stars and politicians. I also make the distinction between scholars and teachers, where the first are studious intellectuals bent on discovery and improvement, and the latter are both gifted to inspire others to learn, and inclined toward the dissemination of knowledge, which may or may not be of their own discovery. Both are commendable in their respective service to society, but with the difference that teachers have a more direct relationship with individual growth, as role-models and instruments of society's influence.

Being a teacher is above all a calling and it has numerous rewards, yet a truly enlightened society should regard the act of teaching as one of the utmost importance and responsibility; thus affording it special dignity. This is so, for a teacher is the agent responsible for nurturing a process that culminates with true social, scientific and economic progress, where the first element results in the second, and both result in the third element. Without a solid foundation in education, no society can hope to ever become egalitarian, productive and sustainable.

Professional educators should therefore be celebrated and remunerated as much for their technical competence as for their dedication and zest for teaching, for on their skill lies much of future discoveries and practical enterprising. Teachers should also be selected under the most rigorous of criteria, for with their calling comes the duty to perform and correspond to society's expectations. Furthermore, in order to teach virtues, teachers should embody at least some of them. I daresay teachers should lead public lives and – within reason – be accessible to students and parents, just as politicians should be accessible to the public.

The ideal society should also concede that, though teachers carry on the process of societal construction, the birth of it is at home, in the bosom of families. Education must therefore happen also at home and in terms of passing-on family values consistent with culture and the endurance of virtuous and moral behaviour. The ideal society must acknowledge this and afford parents the time they need to interact with their children, without inviting prejudice to their professional careers. Businesses must recognise that parenting is an important social function, and that it is favourable to a better socioeconomic environment, the ultimate reflection of which is more long-term business sustainability, through socioeconomic stability.

As well as nurturing families and family values, the ideal society would not be one to fight-off religions, but one that accepts them. If not for spiritual motivations – which are in my personal opinion the worthier – civilisation should embrace religions for the role they carry out in proposing moral conduct, self-awareness, personal restraint, overall patience and social good behaviour. The premise of respect for others and selflessness that is present in most religions is of immense social value. This is a treasure an ideal society would learn to encourage and cherish, let alone allow.

In addition, for the virtuous and conscientious individual to grow out of a child, there must exist a consonance between what is valued at home, in school, by society in general and by the business and political environments, but there must also exist a critical appraisal of social principles based on historical, family, personal and civic values.

Here's the role of cultural context, which is to provide plurality of insight into the presentation and understanding of universal themes. This is not to say that it is desirable to sustain an overtly flexible, or relative, viewpoint on such themes, but to foment diversity of analysis based both on heritage and intent; exercising it through rhetoric to achieve common ground. The central maxim therefore remains untouched, but its interpretation and application would be permeable to personal scrutiny, culture and context, insofar as it would be possible to do so without depriving the parts involved of mutual satisfaction, and without corrupting the essence of the theme.

In so doing, such a society would be teaching its constituent citizens to bear themselves honourably and, at the same time, to peer into one another's mind to seek an understanding. The process would nurture open-mindedness through experience and information; as opposed to social imposition. By the time they reached maturity, youths would indeed mature in the sense that they would not only come of age, but also grow in wisdom.

Here is the basis not only of an orderly and tolerant society, but also of a strong and informed public, capable of carrying out great decisions, and partaking more actively and effectively on local and national politics.

But what of politics itself? How should the ideal society structure public administration? I, for one, do not have the competence to elaborate an entire system of government. Yet I may dream of one. So, without going into too much detail on the subject of system of government, suffice to say that an ideal society should have more plural and more reliable leadership.

This is to say, among other things, that instead of one head of state, a triumvirate may be more conducive to fairness and incorruptibility. The components of a triumvirate should, in all aspects, be equitable and able in their powers. Two of the members should be elected via a direct democratic process, and the third via an indirect vote cast by the elected executive and legislative representatives of the people, including the two directly elected members of the triumvirate. This third member should serve as a catalyst to a functional government and a conciliator of oppositions.

The trio should remain in office for a pre-set term of no more than five years – and I say there is a good number – during which any one member of the triumvirate could be individually substituted, at any time, given sufficient cause in incompetence, corruption or inability to perform, or else given sufficient public refute. Re-election of a same trio should at all times be impossible. Even so, individual members of a triumvirate should be eligible for a new term alongside two other figures. This would hinder corruption, whilst promoting the inclusion of experienced heads of government into new terms of rule.

Apart from personal aides, the cabinet and ministers of the triumvirate should be a shared body, and should enjoy the support of all three heads of government; meaning they all agree on who will occupy the ministries and offices of government.

Whatever the case may be, leaders and heads of state should enjoy ample moral grounds in order to lead. Candidates should at all times be free of any legal impediments. No person with a criminal conviction on file should be allowed to partake in government, even if their debt to society had already been paid. Leadership should remain a privilege reserved for those of exemplary conduct.

As elections go, I always thought a *"vote for"* was insufficient to express a democratic opinion. Better it would be that we each had one *"vote for"* and *"one vote against"* to express both the one person we wish to be in power, and the one we would rather see away from it.

In the ideal society, despite the concept of the triumvirate for the supreme leadership, I submit that each citizen should have the right to these two votes at each election. As well, these should be direct votes, and not collegial or district votes to be pursued indirectly. In that manner, internal governmental compromises, would be minimised. In the end, even at lower echelons of government, it would become easier to compose a functional and unobstructed governing body, for elected officials and legislators would tend to be more cohesive in ideals and proposals, and more consonant with the public that elected them.

Moreover, assuming a democratic regime, and assuming and informed people, we should grant the public a more direct voice; most of all in municipal affairs, but also in national laws affecting them. This would both permit a sense of greater exercise of democracy by a nation's constituents, and it would promote greater transparency in governmental dealings. Indeed, such a form of direct democracy is already present and functional in some countries, and more prominently so in Switzerland, where the model seems to be very productive.

Naturally, it can be argued that small countries like Switzerland provide for easier governance, allowing for greater public participation without expressive practical complications. The fact remains that, given large populations and more complex governmental bodies, it still seems impractical to have a direct democracy, where the constituents would vote on every crucial issue, via a referendum.

Nevertheless, technology already appears to allow society to dream of greater inclusion of direct public opinion on crucial matters affecting a people. The concept of Electronic Direct Democracy – also known as Direct Digital Democracy – proposes the use of telecommunications facilities to promote greater public participation in politics and legislation. Though not yet instituted anywhere in the world, at least as far as I am aware, and the dangers of electronic manipulation of the outcome notwithstanding, experiments are in course to test the notion. I, for one, have little doubt that a serviceable technical solution is achievable.

However, if we set aside the technical aspects of the notion, and if we assume that it is possible and viable to create a means for a permanent system for collecting public opinion, it seems clear to me that, in an ideal society, any candidate law affecting the population in general should be pre-approved, by a significant portion of that population, in a virtual referendum, before it could be voted for sanction by legislative and executive representatives.

In this manner, candidate laws should all be made public via printed and electronic means, so that the interested citizens could voluntarily verify them, and personally reject it or petition it be sanctioned. Each district and electorate should have the ability to hold, at an official building, the infrastructure to display candidate laws, with their justifications, to any citizen wishing to examine them. Holding the ability to display the same information electronically – with access enabled via the World Wide Web – is clearly something already viable, as is proven by the existence of electronic world-spanning social-networks, where polls are regularly taken. Furthermore, in addition to a centralised public service for the availability of the text of the candidate laws and the official arguments for and against it, legislative representatives could, in effect, use their public web-logs and web-sites to further the same end, as some of them already do.

The informed public could then consult these means to verify prospective laws and bills, and then cast a vote for or against it, where every vote against could cancel a vote for, so that the bill is left with a balance indicating the will of the people. This could occur in a predetermined time-frame, or automatically upon reaching a majority vote; which would in effect also indicate the priorities given by the public in general.

At that point, if the bill had a significant positive balance, it could then be voted by legislators, who would necessarily become responsible for scrutinising the legal and technical aspects of the bill, and would also become accountable for their contribution to the sanctioning of the law before the public, as they knew the decision of the people beforehand. It is important to clarify that a legislator could still chose to vote against the will of the people, but the justification for such a vote would necessarily have to be convincing in order for that legislator to be eventually re-elected.

I imagine the process could function more or less in the following manner:

I. A legislator – delegate or senator – proposes a candidate law, and submits it to the public, carefully supporting the proposal with textual facts and figures;

II. During the new law's term of candidacy, a legal body concomitantly verifies the proposal to be legal and constitutional, posting its findings to the public along with the bill itself;

III. The media and other private institutions will be free to dissect the proposal and divulge their findings;

IV. The public in general also accesses the candidate law and examines it, interrogating the proponent and requesting clarification, if need be, and then voluntarily expresses approval or disapproval of it;

V. If by the pre-set due date of the law's candidacy the proposal fails to attract sufficient public attention – say 30% votes both for and against – it is neglected, or perhaps automatically discarded, and doesn't even go to the legislative and executive bodies for analysis;

VI. However, if at any time a candidate law receives palpable public attention – say 30% or more voting citizens vote either for or against – it may be sent to the assembled legislative body for further perusal and backing, and then, if approved, it would go to the executive body for the final endorsement or veto;

VII. Similarly, if a candidate law meets with majority disapproval of the public by its candidacy deadline – with possibly more than 50% of votes are against the bill – it is automatically referenced for final executive examination with a recommendation to veto;

VIII. Equally, a candidate law that reaches majority public approval at any time during its candidacy – say 51% of pertinent population votes for – also automatically moves into executive analysis with a recommendation for final endorsement;

IX. The legislative and executive bodies would respectively be bound to deliberate eligible candidate laws per the order of public attention they received, prioritising those that received more total votes over those that received less;

X. Public approval or disapproval would not bind public powers to following the public appraisal, but it would clearly indicate the will of the people, whereby a delegate, senator, mayor, governor or a triumvirate member – as the case may be – would find it easier to envision what is desired of him or her;

XI. Once approved by the legislative body, the executive body or both, and without any impediment interposed by the legal body, a candidate law would be enacted and incorporated.

In such a system, it would become more difficult to overwhelm the legislative, legal and executive bodies with a great number of candidate laws undergoing morose deliberations, as laws would go to them only after public scrutiny and generally with an indication of what the public wants. It would also become more difficult to enact laws that the public deems unsound or problematic.

Another useful by-product of such a system would indeed be that the legislators' ability to legislate in self-service would be reduced, as the system would contemplate a means of enabling a public voice, directly manifested, prior to decisions affecting the legislators themselves. For instance, the voting on benefits and salaries for members of government would never be handled by themselves alone. It would also be the case that the voting of budgets and benefits for public officers, and matters concerning oligarchies would scarcely take precedence over the voting of laws of genuine and direct public interest.

Such a system of popular referendums, although arguably still expensive and time-consuming, would be conducive to generating a more conscientious and educated civil community, as well as a more philanthropic government. It would also require more information be openly shared by governments with the people they govern, which can only be seen as something positive.

Whereas emergency measures, diplomatic issues, military decisions and the like would still be required to be handled by proxy, by the representatives of the people, in the ideal society, more long-term civil issues should be submitted to popular understanding and scrutiny prior to legislative voting. Only when significant popular approval is manifested for a candidate bill would it actually be submitted to the assembled legislators for voting, and then to the executive branch for final sanctioning. Coupled together, these measures have the potential for generating a fairer and more democratic system.

Also worthy of notice is that those laws voted on an emergency or contingency basis should have limited validity – perhaps a maximum of one year's time – and should become null within a fixed and non-renewable number of days, at which point a permanent law – one devised and submitted to the people via the regular means – would override the emergency measure.

Impractical as it may sound, it should be viable with current technology to address the issues of electoral fraud and electoral expediency with biometrics and computerised sorting of results. I also submit that direct voting should always be a voluntary civil act, as opposed to a compulsory one. In that manner, voters would more naturally happen that are involved with the matters at hand and the politics surrounding them.

All this goes to show that the ideal society would see public service with slightly different eyes than we currently do. It seems to me that there would be a lot more public service involved in public offices, and a lot less self-interest and fringe benefits; though dignity of the offices themselves should remain untarnished. This, in my mind, is favourable to attracting a vaguely different profile of people into public office.

As well, it seems to me that in such an enlightened society, public officers – especially legislators and members of executive bodies – should at all times be bound to have their children attending public schools and universities, and themselves benefiting only from public hospitals and public transportation, as a means of connecting them to the reality of the people.

Another factor that would connect elected officials to the reality of the people they govern is to make the public station itself something more akin to voluntary work than to a profession. This would mean that, where possible, elected officials would necessarily still hold professional careers outside of politics, from which they should derive their principal source of income, with their public service affording them honorary and repository earnings only. The concept may perhaps apply more to legislative officials than to executive officials and judges of the courts, but it is tested and it is sound.

What's more, benefits and salaries to public servants should at all times be proportional to the progress of the national economy, and should automatically be corrected to befit growth and retraction of same. It is my firm belief today that, if governments were to be committed at all with the people they govern, the salaries and benefits of government officials, ministers and top management in governmental institutions, should at all times be proportional to both the country's GDP and the performance of their respective institutions. In that manner, they would grow or shrink as a function of how well they are managing the nation.

If their reward is directly proportional to the performance of the country's economy, it should follow then, that they would take great care to select only people of competence to occupy positions of leadership, and that a country's leaders would police one another in order that one's ineptitude would not affect another's diligent work. It may also follow that the people's perception of their leaders would improve knowing that they are as directly affected by the welfare of the nation as the regular working people. As to corruption in public service, it would certainly endure given the inability of this system to root it out entirely, but the cost of it to the people would be diminished.

Taken together, these measures would lead both to a guarantee of good public facilities, as well as to the attracting of more altruistic profiles into political service. Thus, it would come to pass that the ideal society would be led by idealists and statesmen more than by professional politicians.

Where Law is concerned, again I don't have the technical background to establish a complete system, but the abstractive reasoning remains that can issue an opinion. To me, communal and cohesive as the ideal society should be, it should still have a body of professional judges and a corps of enforcers to protect the public, police and carry-out law enforcement duties. This body should be adequately sized, superbly well equipped, fairly remunerated and properly educed, trained and supported to pursue their demanding duties and to imprint state presence with propriety.

Even in an ideal society, we need to accept that a deviant percentage of the population will exist that will still pursue inequity, wickedness and violence; whereupon it becomes necessary to constitute public powers to address these issues, both in the criminal and civil spheres.

However, in an ideal society, the powers of this corps of enforcers must also have clear-cut limits. The legal body of magistrates and enforcers must have a profound understanding of, and be bound by, due process. There can be no arbitrary infringement of civil rights and privacy, under any ordinary circumstance. There can be no invasive or aggressive police action without solid basis in probable cause. There has to exist unwavering civic accountability, even under extraordinary circumstances. Such is the price of democratic freedom.

As well, in a society of conscience, liability and of prudence, there can be no reason why the civilian population could not be equipped for self-defence, and for the defence of family and of neighbours and of the nation itself, as this option could prove to be useful also in reducing crime. A well-educated and self-aware population, with awareness also of the danger posed by the criminal element, would be conscientious of the danger and responsibility of bearing arms; thus being eligible to bear them, within reasonable restrictions.

Besides, too often have certain governments in history abused the fact that the state is equipped and the common people are not. Alertness to the possibility of the rise of dictatorial regimes would further justify the existence of a civil militia. Such a community should be prepared both to protect self and family, and to uphold and support a free democracy.

It should be the duty of every able adult to learn how to bear arms and/or to learn how to provide ambulatory first-aid and responsible assistance in case of need. Recycling programmes for such skills, principally first-aid, should be administered similarly to driving licences to any citizen, who elected to own a firearm or drive a private conveyance.

The price to pay for the ability to defend oneself against crime with deadly force – or to form a militia against tyranny or invasion – is responsibility. Severe laws should exist to punish misconduct, but not to tarnish the right to self-defence; after all, the criminal element will not bind itself to a ban on private ownership of arms.

For this reason among others, in the criminal sphere, lenience should be permitted to first offenders and to the perpetrators of misdemeanours, but it should be used sparingly where citizens insist on criminal behaviour even after a conviction.

For grievous crimes, a rule of three should be instituted, where a first criminal offence is treated with leniency, a second with severity and a third without clemency. Repeated convictions should immediately incur loss of voting rights and limitations to privileges of citizenship, such as the right to bear arms or to own personal vehicles, or even the right to a passport and to privacy. Whether or how these could be re-conquered should depend on a plain and irrefutable demonstration by the ex-criminal, that he or she has rejected the path of criminal behaviour to become a productive member of society.

Conversely, punishment on petty crimes should be in the form of social service and forced labour, performed preferably in public areas and public services, that an offender may feel ashamed publicly. Incarceration and loss of civil rights should be applied to graver crimes; in particular to crimes against human life and human dignity. Physical punishment should not be ruled out, particularly where crimes against human dignity are regarded.

Where possible, the intrinsic costs of incarceration should be borne by the convicts themselves, within a self-sufficient apparatus to cultivate and prepare foodstuffs, and to otherwise carry out the day-to-day preservation, needs and affairs of prisons. General maintenance and cleaning should be performed by the inmates as much as possible, as should cooking, painting and other routine chores.

While imprisonment should not endanger the prisoners – or their guards – it should not be devoid of hard work. In order to enable smaller and more controllable facilities, different penal complexes could be responsible for different activities generating complementary goods and services. One would be responsible for all the inmate laundry in the region, another for all the horticultural production, another for all the dairy production and so on.

The by-product of this could be the instilling of a sense of mutual dependability instrumental to the peaceful conduct of these basic affairs. Hopefully, the monitored activity could lead to the cultivation of a more responsible attitude towards the community. Certainly, the physical labour could help in keeping orderly behaviour within the penal complexes.

In the civil sphere, law should be less rigid than in the criminal sphere. It should contemplate intent and context as much as rule of law. Crimes against property and white-collar crimes should mostly be treated in the civil sphere, unless they also had the confirmed potential for human injury, or if the offender poses palpable threat to the community. Cases should only go to court where there had been criminal conduct, or after attempts at negotiation and conciliation had been pursued and exhausted.

There should be no overlapping of sentences between the civil sphere and the criminal sphere, as the nature and consequences of the offences and of disputes seem to be contrasted at a quintessential level. Penalties in the civil sphere should be in the form of service to be rendered – privately or publicly – or material compensation. Incarceration should be reserved to heinous and capital crimes against the public and the individual.

In all legal things, the letter of the law should serve principally as a guideline for judges and jury. Both personal conscience – aligned with an understanding of virtues, like justice and honesty – and testimony of character and of circumstances should offer subsidy for its interpretation, in the light of common customs and uses. What's more, an appeal should always be allowed to the parts involved, but never without sufficient cause and never more than twice on any given case, where the first would happen at an equal level and the second to higher constituted authority.

At all times the affairs of the legal system should remain public. Privacy of personal cases and the persons involved in them aside, the other dealings of public courts and of legal decisions on public cases should remain available to verification.

Similarly, judges, public prosecutors and policemen should be submitted to random periodic psychoanalytical scrutiny and financial investigation, as a norm. The dignity of their position notwithstanding, theirs is a public office, and the public should be entitled to ascertain that their ethical, moral and professional standpoints have not been compromised. That the examination would be randomly assigned would make it more impartial and just. What's more, being automatic and random, no moral onus would be attached to such superficial probes. Naturally, unless findings pointed to irregularities, no intrusive investigation on personal affairs should occur.

Likewise, in an accountable ideal society, legal consultants should be co-responsible with their clients if it should be so proven that their clients are intentional criminals, and that such lawyers have defended them knowingly and without a plea of guilty. In these cases, it remains the obligation of lawyers to offer the best possible defence to their clients, but it becomes their duty not to deceive the courts and the public in so doing.

Sociologically speaking, the ideal society would be one of immense social acceptance, inclusion and patience. Tolerance in this society should come as a result of the Golden Rule and the cultivation of personal virtues, and not imposed by minority movements and the like.

Imposed tolerance, even if legally imposed, is distortive and it generates further conflict. The ideal society would be one that arrives at a state of racial, gender, religious and economic tolerance naturally – through education, information and innate disposition toward mutual respect – and not by means of demagogic laws imposed by groups within the state, or under social and moral intimidation from raging rights groups. Intolerance will be minimised by the valorisation of the individual based on how they bear themselves and by the virtues of justice, dignity, prudence, philanthropy and valour.

Correspondingly, the ideal society cannot exist without open-mindedness and patience in face of diversity. Personal choices and natural differences must be acknowledged under the principles of conscience and common sense. The understanding that we are equal in dignity, if we bear ourselves with equal honour, must be the catalyst of tolerance, in spite of any differences. The Golden Rule must be the moral deterrent of any injustice practised out of naked prejudice.

As well the ideal society would be conscientious of the necessity of fomenting philanthropy, both on a public and on a private level. Achievement with selfless results would be prized over success with only personal results.

Society in general would acknowledge the fact that it can only be as great and progressive as the least of its citizens. Society would be aware that fomenting the spread of general welfare has a return impact on the overall quality of life for the entire community. Nevertheless, this cannot be done at the price of accepting indolence as a way of life, even for a portion of society. Effort and dedication should be the duty of every citizen and the response to every act of charity.

The public would indulge equality and meritocracy as means of generating progress. The general gender would value equal opportunity, via fair distribution of wealth, if it resulted from consistent investment in good education and in free access to public facilities. Rulers would acknowledge that it is better to be a poor public officer ruling over a rich people, than the opposite.

Schools, technical education programmes and universities should be bestowed with ample support from both public and private sectors, including a mutually beneficial exchange between companies and apprentices, via trainee programmes, especially if such educational institutions awarded significant scholarships to the community, or if they were operated by the state. The state itself should promote such programmes within its various institutions to set the example.

Moreover, if they could prove their skills with documental evidence or before a technical commission, incentives should be given for experienced artists, artisans, entrepreneurs and technicians venturing in the marketplace, to pursue careers at which they excel. This would be requested by the applicants under the obligation to pass-on their expertise to the next generation. Public-sector inducements would come to those with proven skill, via grants and loans at low interest rates, or with temporary tax exemption for the development of activities related with those proven skills, wherever they would result in benefits to the public in general and to underdeveloped social groups.

Coaching programmes to generate an increase in technical skill among the population could be developed thus, with professionals that receive public grants necessarily being assigned apprentices who would work for them, receive payment – allotted either from the grants themselves or from natural profits where applicable – and also learn the profession and become qualified.

The larger the enterprise being supported with state assistance, the more apprentices it would be charged with for training and refining into productive skilled professionals. Inevitably, this system of apprenticeship would be monitored by the state, who would assume the role of sponsor and regulator, both to foment new productive activity and to guarantee that state loans are being used adequately by the businesses, and also to educate trainees competently and without abuse.

Cultural activity would be indulged by our ideal society and could enjoy lowering of taxation over projects that involved the arts, insofar as these projects were made accessible to the general public, via popular pricing. While access to libraries, museums, shows and presentations should not necessarily be free of charge, they could all perhaps forgo a basis in inflated admissions, prohibitive royalties, bloated fees and salaries; as are sometimes practised in show business. Where abuses were obstinately perpetrated, the state would intervene with fines or heavy taxation, so that it would become more attractive to make shows affordable to the masses than to exclusive audiences.

Handmade goods, products involving arts and crafts or copyright could meet with the same criterion, and be eligible for reduced taxation, as long as this facility resulted in pricing advantageous to the general public. While artisans would be able to market their products at attractive pricing – becoming able to make a living out of their crafts, despite competition from industrial goods – the sale of books, music, software and other intellectually proprietary material could as well become more affordable. This would both coerce the practice of intellectual piracy and restrain abusive royalties to make handmade goods, art, literature and music more attractive to every person.

Sport should also have its prominent place in society, but within proportion. While amateur leagues should encounter more incentives and be more widely indulged, as a means of complementing education and promoting a good state of health, professional sport should meet with a divorce from excessive involvement with sponsorships, betting and from exorbitant salaries to star players.

The ideal society would frown upon excesses associated to sport, because such excesses compromise the purity of the activity itself. Let players be paid in accordance with what they do. Let their dignity come from the sport and how they practice it. Let the public admire them for what they do and represent. Let sponsorships participate insofar as providing infrastructure and equipment to the sports and teams as a whole. Let active sportsmen refrain from celebrity endorsements they are not qualified to make. Let not money speak too loudly for the decisions of coaches and leagues.

What of the economics of the ideal society? Firstly, I'd say that intervention by the state in day-to-day affairs of economic activity, industry, markets and the commercial activities of society in general should be relegated principally to the role of regulator. The state should be like a silent watchman, not a knight in shiny armour on a rowdy courser. The state should indicate policy and point to danger and intervene to prevent abuse. It should not meddle in markets.

Ideally, the state should deal in the establishing of infrastructure and grounds for private-sector success, and it should attend to establishing a sound business environment;

no more and no less. It should not intrude with bail-out aid to re-establish a balance where there was none to begin with. The state should not flood the market with funds to prevent collapse of companies and systems that have already failed on their own.

The reason why I affirm this is that, in so doing, the state is preventing the consequences of certain acts by protecting their causes. In effect, such interventions tend to promote further failure; not prevent it. Whenever the state intrudes in such manner, it is indeed averting that a flaw in the system be self-corrected by the outcome of its corruption.

No deregulated market should exist that would invite greed and abuse. Likewise, no free market can exist where the state uses public funds to control market prices, availability of credit and the rates of currency in international commerce. These controls, when made by the state, should follow the rule of laws enacted publicly and clearly to deter abuse. Public funds should in all matters be used directly for the benefit of the public, by financing public infrastructure, education, issues of public health and social parity, and for the up-keeping of public institutions; not for the defence of oligarchies and private enterprise.

Under this premise, the ideal global society should establish a commercial and industrial system of cooperative and interdependent micro-economies. By this I mean we should strive to limit the influence of domineering corporations over markets, and place our emphasis and incentives into small, more specialised and localised businesses, existing in greater diversity.

By the term *"domineering corporations"* please understand I mean large and vertical multinational conglomerates, operating under the principle of supreme profits, as previously discussed in other chapters. I do not mean public and private enterprises with great financial power or public monopolies with the responsibility to provide infrastructure and services, for the benefit of society in general.

The dynamics of local businesses allow for greater familiarity with the surrounding community and immediate identification with it and its direct needs, attributing greater rapport between the institution and the community. Additionally, smaller companies operating in segmented and niche markets tend to acquire greater specialisation and excellence specific to their geography and activity. Add to this the ingredient of mutual dependability and outsourcing may well become the rule to provide more opportunity and greater diversification between companies and the solutions they offer.

This is not to say that products could not be produced in one place and then shipped to another – even across the globe – but simply that the incentives should exist for a plurality of sources rather than one great monopoly, operating with global market barriers, to make it the supreme source of one thing or another.

By all means, if there is a company that expertly manufactures a particular industrial item like no other, let it be successful and export its product to any willing customer, within or outside the nation. Likewise, let a country that is born and bred to provide quality foodstuffs export its produce into other markets, unbarred by artificial barriers. Simply make sure that the exchange happens naturally and without artificial economic devices and customs barriers to distort it.

What's also important where global sources are regarded is to establish criteria demanding that imported goods be generated under the same ethos of fair business practices and labour codes than those of the ideal society itself. This would conscientiously prevent that product be generated under realities incoherent with, or depreciative of the values of, the ideal society and then shipped into it to compete with products that abided by the ideal ethical code.

Naturally, there is a price to pay. In this scenario, it is probable that smaller production scale afforded by the microeconomic model would tend toward making products more expensive. Nonetheless, with competition based solely on cost-reduction being excluded as a predominant factor, and with fairer and more proportional pricing levels being practised across the markets, according to intrinsic and added value – e.g., infrastructure and expertise involved in production, offer & demand, and actual delivery of benefits – there would be grounds for an improvement in overall quality of products and efficiency of services.

Competition would be prone to occur not in detriment of quality, but as a function of it. Needless to say, this is a gain both social and technological, as it would be instrumental in establishing a system that would remunerate workers better and as a function of performance.

This means that, if we attribute just value to both quality and efficiency in marketable products, we should see, as a by-product of that system, the individual employee becoming more endowed of means to spend. If indeed more expensive product translated into wealthier and more satisfied employees, we should see a better distribution of wealth and an improvement to equality of opportunity. This would, in effect, mean that companies would be able to rely on a greater diversity of customers and more stable markets. In the long-term, the industry would benefit from a divorce from cost-reduction competition.

Even so, realistically speaking, we should see slower expansion of profits and markets, with stability prevailing over growth. To me, the ideal society should take this to be an improvement over rampant consumerism, as it probably provides for a better entrepreneurial environment. Slower and more stable economies invite an atmosphere where long-term and more responsible planning becomes more viable. This scenario would also bring about a situation where we can manage environmental issues more easily.

The economy of the ideal society should contemplate ecological concerns more seriously and maturely, because it is better equipped for such considerations. Among other things, the revising of a power matrix based primarily on fossil fuels should be seen not as an economic burden, but as an opportunity to reinvest in infrastructure and generate new technologies, the consequence of which would be the creation of new temporary jobs and new perennial careers.

Envision what ripples in society and technology a national or global investment on a new power matrix could bring. Picture what the investment in renewing the power distribution infrastructure would generate in opportunity for employment and for reimagining our world. Imagine its mid-term benefits in redistribution of wealth and in the fostering of social justice. Imagine the long-term benefits to the environment and to quality of life. In the selfless ideal global society, such an endeavour would be coveted heartily.

Ideally, all this should be pursued openly and with the virtues that guide the ideal society always in mind. Never could a society made from men and women that compromise their virtues and their conscience achieve such herculean goals. In essence, personal conscience should guide every public officer and every citizen.

Also, where there is a critical mass of people desirous of being honest and generally honourable, there is where commercial relationships become uncomplicated and agile. Imagine, if you will, a commercial structure where you can contact a supplier with an urgent request, and that supplier can muster resources to answer to your company's needs, without any guarantee of compensation being required for mobilisation, other than your word that you will make good on your material obligations upon delivery.

Now imagine that you can also trust your supplier to deliver as promised and within specifications simply because they are committed to that purpose. The supplier will not underestimate his lead-time. He will not overestimate his quality. He will state his ability to supply your needs, and will fulfil it accordingly.

Taken together these two realities would make possible more rapid responses and an unencumbered commercial and financial system. Is that not an environment vigorously to be wished? Is this not worth giving up short-term profits and undue advantages? It sounds obvious, but it doesn't feel like this is what predominantly occurs in the global markets at this time.

The principal price for such a scenario is the prevalence of individual rectitude, after which organisational and mercantile candour necessarily follow. The collateral price is that the supplier must be adequately rewarded both materially and socially. In other words, if the price is fair, it must be paid on time and without subterfuge, and it will because it would not be just to proceed otherwise. If quality is superlative, it should be rewarded monetarily, though not excessively so, and should receive ample support via referencing. Added efficiency or more stringent requirements should always have an impact on pricing. No other explanation should be required.

If, for instance, requested lead-time is shorter than usual, additional fees should be applicable to achieve the feat because the additional cost had not been computed in the regular pricing. Conversely, complete fulfilment of an agreement and all its inherent promises, under whatever terms, should be expected and granted without ado.

This may all seem obvious in principle, but in reality – our reality – they are more often than not compromised by the pressures and the objectives already widely discussed in previous chapters. In the ideal society, businessmen intrinsically know that there is no place for malice and subterfuge in such a commercial system as the one proposed here. Likewise, there is no place for undue price depreciation, the pursuit of unfair commercial advantages or disloyal competition.

If sellers resort to these practices, if buyers indulge them and if managers reward them, the system is corrupted. It only works up until it is consistently abused. At that point, it reacts to protect itself to the detriment of all. In the ideal society, businessmen on both ends of the bargain do not seek undue advantages; for they realise that only mutually sustainable business is good business.

Can the ideal society exist? Search yourself and you will know an honest enough answer. For my part, I dare dream that it could, for the impediments to it are of our own making, and as such they can be supplanted by us.

* * * * * * *

Chapter IX

CHANGING THE WORLD
& RESISTING THE CHANGE

Resistance to change is natural in any social group. No matter how open minded we say we are, most of us feel that there is a proper way to do things, and we rely on habits and customs to tell us what the meaning of *"proper"* really is. This resilience to modifying things is even more evident, when there is a perception of comfort and benefit in a significant portion of the group, or within the dominant stratum of that group. It is not so much a logical thing as it is a matter of instinct. Such is our case.

On the other hand, change is prompted mainly by discomfort and by substantial dissatisfaction. Mild changes and adjustments are more often suggested or imposed by forces ruling society than they are a fruit of popular desire. In contrast, revolutions – which we should understand here as comprehensive change – historically come more frequently from the base of a social group than from its apex.

This is very logical, as the ruling stratum of any society is often the one that benefits the most from the status quo it helped into existence. What this means is that, without comprehensive popular support, or failing that strength coming from legitimacy or sheer brute force, widespread change is very difficult to implement.

This is one of the reasons the present model is so ingenious. The changes that have been leading us here happened gradually – sometimes nearly unnoticeably – and via the subversion of popular opinion. Society of the present is the fruit of a process that begun with the Industrial Revolution, and that picked up the pace with the more recent introduction of consumerism as the maxim of the entire population. The hegemonies at the headship of the system – which by no means are a cohesive and unchangeable group – are quite secure in their position, for the general gender has come to agree with their proposition; generally hoping to become them at some point.

More to the point, while nowadays there are already significant groups of dissatisfied members of our contemporary global society, there is no single unifying factor for their dissatisfaction. Quite the contrary, there are deep divisions among discontented groups ranging from differences in social, historical, ethnical, behavioural and goal standpoints.

Large portions of our Global society are justifiably discontented with regards to their basic material needs. Other groups are just malcontent in their level of wealth or influence. There are many those also who identify all their problems with not having ascended in the present socioeconomic order. Of these, there are some that acknowledge the existing problems, but are not concerned with resolving these problems as much as simply avoiding them through social ascension and material wealth. Several are disgruntled about the way governments and institutions conduct the different affairs of our global group, but they can't agree on which factors should be resolved first. There's concern for the environment. There is concern for civilisation. There is concern for economies.

In other words, discontentment abounds worldwide, yet there is no unison in identifying the motives and reasons for such dismay. No group identity exists that unifies all these fears and unfulfilled needs and desires. It sometimes seems that the world is united in grief and at odds about what causes it and what tempers our collective heartache. Herein is our shared problem in addressing these causes.

By the present date, it is perceptible that many people have already realised that the current socioeconomic model of our society is inherently flawed, and utterly unsustainable, in the social, economic and environmental sense of the term. However, these are a significantly small crowd in global terms. Most of global society is still concerned with more immediate threats such as war, famine, economic survival and social inclusion, which in turn are the source of many of our divisions.

Social and institutional resistance to change is wholly natural, and it has much to do with comfort zones and the social structure of decision making. First and foremost, the system that is in place today exists under a leadership. This hegemony that is present at the top of the current system benefits from that position and defends it. Then there's the fact that we too are too comfortably set about our lives to care about the plight of others; our egotism has been carefully fostered after all. Either that, or we are too busy to care.

What's more, the ingenuity of the present model, its relative historical success and the mechanics of its workings are ultimately the tools of the status quo. Without going into the specifics of whether or not this is a deliberate process, and to which extent it could or could not be, it is quite clear that the effectiveness and the seduction of the ethos of profit, through consumerism, will continue to prevail for at least a generation; more likely several.

The fostering of human greed and of human insatiability via the detachment from perennial moral values, and as a function of an economy based on the unrealistic premise of continual growth has, in effect, caused important distortions both in national and global economies, their financial systems, their commercial and consumer relationships, and to the very fabric of national societies. Consequently, the system creating these distortions is destined to implode as a result of them; not least of which is the decay of ethical behaviour in all forms of human interaction. What remains to be seen is how and when.

Yet, if the realisation that important flaws exist and produce consequences is insufficiently strong to promote a change of paradigm, where would the world find the motivation to change?

The successions of economic crises that have transpired in the last decades, and that persist to-date, have unequivocally pointed to the need for re-examination of our model. The various crises indicate – among other things – that artificial devices within the economies of nations, which themselves are connected by a global system, are in place to attempt to impose a financial component of control over free trade, which in effect distorts the dynamics of global free enterprise and global competition. What should happen on a basis of predisposition, competence and quality actually happens on a basis of politics, influence, power – both hard and soft – and capital. However, the distortions that these controls cause in terms of promoting barriers to free trade are pale when compared to the fabricated duplication of monetary facilities based principally – if not exclusively – in financial credibility.

What I mean is that other devices exist that are present primarily to promote an unrealistic and dangerous multiplication of capital, unfolding into subsequent and multifaceted intangible formats. In the final analysis, this insubstantial wealth exists to serve the purpose of fomenting continually growing profits where in fact there should be none.

Along with non-productive sources of wealth and fictitious money, we also have the pressure for growth generating a lowering of ethical behaviour and common sense, in both financial and commercial relationships, which in effect translates into fraud, embezzlement and other white-collar crimes becoming widely put into practice. That this is a self-crippling process should become evident again soon enough. That it is harmful to the ecology and to society is already quite plain. Yet a more general acknowledgement is still required, due to the resilience of the prevailing oligarchies more than to the will of the people, who may not be sensitive to the times, but who are immensely pliable at present.

The main problem remains that the elusive wealth resulting from all these devices is funnelled principally into global hegemonies that will do everything in their power to keep the status quo. That it spills into the pockets of the emergent middle class aggravates the scenario, in that the middle class will also resist the change. That the fictitious wealth does not leak into the base of society with any relevance may be an opportunity for redemption, for they have not yet been wholly contaminated by it. Still, everyone is connected by the negative ripples that the successive global economic crises have been causing.

This is an interesting scenario in that *"everything within the power of the hegemonies"* may actually mean a re-evaluation of the system itself; possibly to result in a more stable and less harmful proposition. The older model of generational wealth and power may yet prove to be more advantageous to society in general, and to the planet itself, than our *"novel"* model of instant affluence. A genuinely new model – although less likely – also becomes possible.

Faced with the present and looking into a gloomy future, contemporary hegemonies may come to realise that wealth based on non-productive activity should essentially be limited by wealth that does generate tangible benefits for the main reasons that it can last much longer, employ more people and spread the wealth further throughout global society.

While today it is quite obvious that non-productive profitability is immensely rewarding – often even more rewarding than productive activity – the evidence that, in effect, speculative profit is one of the root causes of the successive economic busts the world has been experiencing, may create sufficient unison between and among social strata to prompt a change.

In essence, on one hand we have a tardy but mounting awareness of the imperfection of the prevailing socioeconomic system, and the alertness to the fact that ethics in certain central institutions has been compromised to a dangerous level. On the other, we have a very powerful, proven and warped system still feeding off the greed it implanted into society in general. A change will necessarily come. Whether it will be a change for the better or for worse remains to be seen. There is good reason for hope.

The forces for change are, at this point, indubitably feebler, and less organised than, the inertia existing under the premise of prevalence of consumer relationships and the ethos of profit. We have, after all, been fomenting this situation for a very long time. The present generation, like the one before it, has grown up used to the way things are at present, and habit is a strong force in its own right.

Be that as it may, we are living a unique historical moment. It is unique because it has the potential to generate quintessential social change instead of just a change of leadership. It is a singular moment of but a few such historical periods, where different social classes are united in the inconveniences of the imbalance of society and their consequences to planetary ecology. We live at a time when we may finally realise that the relative wealth of many is better overall than the absolute wealth of a few, even for those few themselves.

The technology and the means to generate a truly global society already exist. This is proven in the way global corporations and global banks have structured themselves to partake in global wealth. What remains to be seen is whether or not we will begin to act as a global society, concerning ourselves not personally, not locally, not nationally, but internationally to generate a system united in the goal of reaching a more satisfactory balance for every citizen in every nation. It is within our reach to do so. We have just lacked the will to pursue it.

* * * * * * *

Chapter X

FINAL CONSIDERATIONS

I will end this book as I have begun it by saying that I don't own the truth; I just borrow it from time to time. Though I don't believe myself incorrect at this point in time – else I would not have written what I wrote – it may well be that others will prove me so.

Similarly, I do not claim to have designed entirely original ideas. Even though I have arrived at these concepts mostly out of my own imagination, I admit I am neither as learned nor as well informed as to claim that they were never imagined before me. I present them here with no such claim as to make them solely my own, but indeed with the desire to share them and offer them to any, who would embrace them and improve on them, with technical propriety.

I want to make it clear once again that I do not think that every person and every human relationship is tainted. Neither do I think that it is my place to judge anyone who deems their life should indeed revolve around money, luxury and power. Each to his own, is what I say in such cases. After all, I hold that it is a matter of personal conscience.

Furthermore, I do not accuse every wealthy individual of corruption and frivolity, and I do not feel that every magnate, marketer, advertising profession and banker is the devil incarnate and every consumer a fool.

Hardworking men and women are everywhere that deserve their prosperity, and I shall never propose to take it away from them, nor should anyone else. Good people abound in every profession and position. Besides, there are prudent people and conscientious voices even in unexpected circles, and they have merit above those who are not inserted in adverse environments. There are indeed very ethical, moral and good people in all places and positions and I do not mean to say that there are not.

What I do mean to say is that we have to make these sensible voices heard, even above our individual comforts and personal conveniences, and even at the cost of our desire for material wealth. What I mean to say is that people are much more than what they carry in their wallets, show their neighbours and hide in their bank accounts.

As individuals and as a society, we should not feel threatened by austerity and frugality. We should not be enslaved by material wealth. It's an obvious fact, but also one that we have been taking for granted and even forgetting.

In our forgetfulness, our society has lost its identity, not to progress and invention and not to equality and tolerance – which are all sorely lacking nowadays – but to greed and irresponsibility and profligacy and immorality. We are not better than we were, we are – every one of us – just more corrupt and decadent. We are collectively selling our ecology, our values and our identity, very cheaply, for a little extra gratification and comfort. We have each and all developed a mercenary mind to go with our lack of selflessness, and we dare think we are righteous in it.

At the age of globalisation, the first things to become global have been greed, unaccountability, usury and inequity. What's more, if there are those who are to blame for our collective social decay, then blame befalls equally on anyone corrupting and anyone letting themselves be corrupted. At the end of the day, we are what we want to be.

Therein is my grievance with the rapid changes we have been witnessing over the past decades. As a society, we have become complacent and inert, and those are unforgivable traits in a species that dominates a planet and dreams to venture beyond it.

We boast our great technological advancement and we shout the glories of our modern society, but in the end, we have sacrificed our very freedoms – indeed our humanity and our conscience – to achieve all this, and it may have been best that we had not done it quite in that way.

Hope remains that we have toiled and that, though many dreams may have been foiled, we are still here to dream new dreams. I submit to you that it is time we dream them hard and far beyond the petty material things with which we surround ourselves.

I invite you to dream of greater glories than driving a fancy car and wearing designer clothes; for these are but artificially expensive items and cheap objectives. Things bigger and wider and greater await your fancy. The world awaits true justice and true equality and unquestionable progress. The nations of the world await true collaboration and lasting peace since the birth of Man. The peoples of the world await the chance to become one people under the common goals of global harmony, coexistence and mutual respect. These things are within our reach. Today. If we work for them.

These are dreams that can come true by our hands and minds put together, but acting individually just as well. Having dreamt the dream, roll up your sleeves and pursue it. Not with anger. Not with hate. Pursue it placidly and constructively and every day. Talk about it. Think about it. Do something about it.

Just as your decisions are always ultimately yours, so is yours the responsibility to make things happen as you want them to be. You, the reader, can do more than you may have imagined just by wishing it so; let alone giving action to your wishes.

You may begin with yourself. Be to others what you want others to be for you. Do to others what you want others to do for you. Keep the Golden Rule. Act per your conscience and never surrender it to fashion. Be strong. Be just. Be honourable and charitable. You don't have to be perfect, but you should try to be better.

Do all this and, rest assured, Humanity's wildest dreams may very well come true in you.

* * * * * * *

ABOUT THE AUTHOR

TOM NOEL-MORGAN is a travelled man, a captivating fellow and a good conversationalist, but he's definitely not what you'd call "typical". He's the kind of person you can't quite label, and he has an accent you can't quite place.

This singularity is perhaps part of the charm that he manages to transfer into his books. Tom has written about non-fiction subjects as diverse as business, politics, religion & philosophy (which he bases on first-hand experience), and also more than a few action-packed genre fiction books (which some will tell you are also based on personal experience, though he denies it).

As a fiction writer, he seems to always find fresh ways of looking at choice themes. As a non-fiction writer, Tom has written serious social criticism, but he admits he has been criticized himself on many occasions. "I feel it is better to be criticized for an honest personal view, than congratulated on dishonestly upholding the politically correct ethos," he says. "The world has enough people adopting mainstream ideas without scrutiny. We need more people to think independently, and then voice their ideas."

His titles include the ongoing "Memoirs of a Zone Raider" series, "Henry Havoc & the Raven Riders", "Universal Utopia", "Morals-Dilemma for the Anesthetised Mind", "7 Original Dice Games" and many others.

* * * * * * *

READ ALSO

TOM NOEL-MORGAN

MORALS DILEMMA FOR THE ANESTHETISED MIND

Individual & Society

* * * * * * *

APPENDIX 1:
END NOTES

[i] Henry David Thoreau. Civil Disobedience. 1848. reprinted Signet Classic, New York. 1960 pp. 228, 229, 236.

[ii] John Dewey – pragmatic philosopher – reportedly asserted that complete democracy was attainable beyond the extension of voting rights but by ensuring the existence of a fully formed public opinion based on effective communication among citizens, specialists, and politicians, with the latter being accountable for the policies they adopt.

[iii] J.C. Harsanyi: "Cardinal utility in welfare economics and in the theory of risk-taking - J. Polit. Economy 61, 1953

[iv] John Rawls: "A Theory of Justice" - Belknap Press, 1971

[v] Sir Isaiah Berlin: "Against the Current: Essays in the History of Ideas" - London: Pimlico, 1997

[vi] John Rawls: "A Theory of Justice"; 1975

[vii] A. H. Maslow was a XX century American professor of psychology at Brandeis University, Brooklyn College, New School for Social Research and Columbia University known for the creation of a concept of hierarchy of needs.

[viii] C. R. Darwin FRS was a XIX century English naturalist known for his Theory of Evolution based on natural selection.

[ix] B. F. Skinner was a XX century American behaviourist, author, inventor, social philosopher and poet known for his study of human behaviour and conditioning.

[x] e.g. *"designed obsolescence"*, also known as *"planned obsolescence"*, *"obsolescence of desirability"* or *"built-in obsolescence"*, which is the strategy of rendering an otherwise functioning device useless either in reality or in the perception of the consumer via a technical, stylistic, aesthetic or otherwise functional or influential basis.

[xi] First noted by Edward Thorndike in the 1920s, the halo effect is a cognitive prejudice involving perception of beauty and quality to influence decisions based not on direct fact but on indirect relationships of perception.

[xii] Keysers, Christian; Gazzola, Valeria (2010). "Social Neuroscience: Mirror Neurons recorded in Humans". Current Biology 20 (8): R353–354. doi:10.1016/j.cub.2010.03.013. PMID 21749952.

[xiii] Senate Financial Crisis Report, April 2011

[xiv] Reuters. September 2009, from Business Wire News database.

[xv] "The US Financial and Economic Crisis: Where Does It Stand and Where Do We Go From Here?" – Brookings; June 2009

[xvi] Zygmunt Bauman is a contemporary Polish sociologist and emeritus professor of the University of Leeds, who is best known for his analyses of postmodern consumerism and the links between the Holocaust and modern society.

[xvii] "Human Universals" - New York: McGraw-Hill, 1991.

[xviii] Such as: Charles Sanders Peirce, William James, John Dewey and George Santayana.

[xix] See the works and comments on Protagoras, Bernard Crick, Paul Feyerabend, L. Ron Hubbard, Robert Nozick, George Lakoff and Mark Johnson

[xx] See the works of Charles Sanders Peirce, William James, John Dewey and George Santayana, among others.
[xxi] Matthew 7:12, see also Luke 6:31
[xxii] Matthew 7:12, see also Luke 6:31
[xxiii] Simon Blackburn is a British academic philosopher advocating quasi-realism and neo-Humean views. Former professor at the University of Cambridge, research professor of philosophy at the University of North Carolina at Chapel Hill, a Fellow of Trinity College, Cambridge, and a member of the professoriate of New College of the Humanities. He is a former president of the Aristotelian society, having served the 2009-2010 term.
[xxiv] 己所不欲，勿施於人
[xxv] 子貢問曰："有一言而可以終身行之者乎"？子曰："其恕乎！己所不欲、勿施於人。"
[xxvi] Brihaspati, Mahabharata - Anusasana Parva, Section CXIII, Verse 8
[xxvii] Suman Suttam , verse 150
[xxviii] Plato's Socrates; Crito, 49c (c. 469 BC–399 BCE)
[xxix] Tobit 4:15
[xxx] Sirach 31:15
[xxxi] Talmud, Shabbat 31a "The Great Principle"
[xxxii] Matthew 7:12
[xxxiii] Luke 6:31
[xxxiv] Luke 10:25-28 "The Great Commandment"
[xxxv] Kitab al-Kafi, vol. 2, p. 146
[xxxvi] An-Nawawi's Forty Hadith 13 (p. 56)
[xxxvii] Sukhanan-i-Muhammad, Teheran, 1938
[xxxviii] p.1299, Guru Granth Sahib
[xxxix] Gertrude Elizabeth Margaret Anscombe was a British analytic philosopher influenced by Ludwig Wittgenstein.
[xl] Charles Darwin. "The Origin of the Moral Sense" in P Singer (ed). Ethics. Oxford University Press. NY 1994 p. 44.
[xli] Quoted in Gino Segre. Faust in Copenhagen: A Struggle for the Soul of Physics and the Birth of the Nuclear Age. Pimlico. London 2007. p. 144.
[xlii] Einstein, A. (1940). "Science and religion". Bibcode 1940Natur.146..605E. doi:10.1038/146605a0. &
[xliii] See the works of Richard Dawkins, Robert Hinde, Michael Shermer, Robert Buckman & Marc Hauser.
[xliv] Peter Albert David Singer is an Australian utilitarian philosopher who is the Ira W. De Camp Professor of Bioethics at Princeton University and Laureate Professor at the Centre for Applied Philosophy and Public Ethics at the University of Melbourne.
[xlv] John Ralston Saul, CC is a Canadian author, essayist, and President of PEN International.
[xlvi] John Ralston Saul. The Unconscious Civilisation. Massey Lectures Series. Anansi Pres, Toronto. 1995. ISBN 0-88784-586-X pp. 17, 81 and 172.
[xlvii] Sam Harris - American author, public intellectual and neuroscientist. Authored books such as "The End of Faith" in 2004, " Letter to a Christian Nation" in 2006, "The Moral Landscape" in 2010, the essay "Lying" in 2011, and the short book "Free Will" in 2012.

Manufactured by Amazon.ca
Bolton, ON